What people are saying about

Clock versus Compass

Find a quiet space, relax and enjoy the clever juxtapositions, insightful comparisons and piercing reflections that all come together in this collection of nuggets of perennial wisdom.
Mike George, author, *Being Beyond Belief*

A witty, accessible and charming book. If you are looking to savor your life, one bite at a time, this just may be the book for you!
Tal Ben-Sharar, author, *Happier; Positive Psychology* lecturer at Harvard University

Clock versus Compass

Art of Positive Balance

Clock versus Compass

Art of Positive Balance

Reena Raj

BOOKS

Winchester, UK
Washington, USA

First published by O-Books, 2019
O-Books is an imprint of John Hunt Publishing Ltd., 3 East St., Alresford,
Hampshire SO24 9EE, UK
office1@jhpbooks.net
www.johnhuntpublishing.com

For distributor details and how to order please visit the 'Ordering' section on our website.

ISBN: 978 1 78535 828 9
978 1 78535 829 6 (ebook)
Library of Congress Control Number: 2017956153

A CIP catalogue record for this book is available from the British Library.

Printed and bound by CPI Group (UK) Ltd, Croydon, CR0 4YY, UK
US: Printed and bound by Edwards Brothers Malloy 15200 NBN Way #B, Blue Ridge Summit, PA 17214, USA

Contents

Introduction

This book presents a unique list of easy to understand bite-sized concepts amalgamated from the fields of applied positive psychology, coaching and spirituality.
It looks at everyday concepts with a view to explore positive balance of real priorities in life.
'Balance' does not get much airplay, as perhaps it does not sound as dynamic or exciting as passion, resilience, transformation, grit, optimism... and amidst these powerful and dynamic notions the appeal of 'balance' is somewhat lost.
Yet, perhaps the real secret to a happy life often lies in the fine balance of things.
Too much passion can turn into obsession, too much resilience can become resistance, too much compassion can turn into gullibility, grit into inflexibility, optimism into blind faith, zest into hyperactivity...
Positive balance doesn't just mean not having too much or too less of something. Positive balance means knowing what is important and when. It means having clarity on life's priorities.

Right balance creates peace and harmony in our lives.
This book goes through some interesting comparisons that are thought-provoking and might help in generating clarity on real priorities in life.

Note: At times it might appear the differences between comparisons are just that of semantics but it is important to look beyond that. It is also important to engage with the suggested activities and exercises in order to promote inner reflection and learning...

Last, there is no particular order and it is perfectly OK to flick through and read any random page.

Mind

Head

Head is the intellect. It reasons and discerns and classifies all the information we receive from the external world.
We all need to apply logic and reasoning in some situations.

Heart

Heart is beyond intellect and reasoning.
It is the deep intuitive sense within.
Sometimes we just 'know' it in our Heart.
This 'knowing' at times goes beyond logic, intellect and reasoning…

Head is the driver and the Heart is the passenger.
Heart needs to give good clear instructions to the driver where to go.
When there is no strong indication from the passenger, the driver drives aimlessly.
After giving clear instructions the passenger should trust the driver to figure out the best route to the destination.
Heart needn't worry about which route to take as long as it knows what the destination is…
Too much worry about the route will stop the Heart from enjoying the journey.
The Head should just focus on driving carefully and vigilantly,
It should stop worrying about what the destination will look like and what will happen when it gets there.
Let the Head drive and let the Heart decide the destination and enjoy the journey.

Wherever you go, go with all your heart.
Confucius

Think about: A past decision where you used your gut feeling instead of reasoning. What went well in relation to that particular decision?

Resources

Resources are time, money, possessions, property, premises... and all sorts of other things and objects...

Resourcefulness

Resourcefulness is creativity, passion, determination, strong will, perseverance... our internal strengths...

Too much importance is placed on first acquiring the resources in order to achieve what you want to achieve. Perhaps... it is better to develop your resourcefulness first.
When you become resourceful you will know how and where to find the resources that you need for achieving your goals.

When we don't cultivate resourcefulness... then even if resources appear in front of us we have no ability to recognize them for what they are.

When there is true resourcefulness it can create and recognize all the resources that are around already.

Think about: Something you achieved recently and then list all the inner qualities you think helped you to achieve that goal.

Microscope

At times we go too much into detail.
Why did this happen? Why did he/she say that? Why is this happening to me?
Why, why, why, why...
We analyse, scrutinize, examine, inspect, dissect, magnify too much... like microscopic vision.

Telescope

With the Telescope we can see far into the sky... gaze at the Stars and the Moon.
With the Telescope we are able to see things that are far, far away... we see the bigger picture.
Telescope is different from the microscope, yet the lens of the Telescope is equally powerful.

Whenever you find yourself ruminating and going in a downward spiral with why why why... swap your Microscope with the Telescope.
Don't spend too much time looking through the Microscope.
Use the Telescope more.
Telescope shows the big picture of what really matters.

Love looks through a telescope; envy, through a microscope.
Josh Billings

Do: Make a list of situations where it is good to use a Telescope.
Example: When I am thinking about a past hurt, perhaps it is better for me to see the bigger picture...

Knowledge

What is knowledge? Knowledge is information.
Information is easily available these days...
Google can provide loads of information on any topic in an instant.
Knowledge is about gaining information about new things.
It is an addition.

Wisdom

What is Wisdom? When we use our knowledge to do the right thing...
Wisdom is not available online.
Information and wise words are...
How we apply the information and wise words in real life is Wisdom.
Wisdom is about letting go of things that are negative.
It is a subtraction.

Wisdom is beyond information, it is about transformation...
Don't be too hung up about knowing everything.
Too much knowledge without wisdom is useless.

To attain knowledge, add things every day.
To attain wisdom, remove things every day.
Lao Tzu

Try this: Don't use Google (or any other search engine) for a day... Next day think about the things you had wanted to look up; how many were actually important?

Judging

Judging is discriminating.
When we see things only from one perspective, we discriminate.
To Judge someone or something is based on bias or blame.
No one likes being judged by someone else...

Discerning

It is good to be discerning.
When we are perceptive and understand things deeply from all angles, we are able to discern with greater and deeper understanding...
Discerning is being perceptive and knowing the difference but without blame.

Discern without judging.

Discernment is not just knowing the difference between right and wrong.
It is knowing the difference between right and almost right.
CH Spurgeon

Think about: Instances when you judged someone and when someone judged you. Recall how it felt in both situations.

Critical Thinking

Critical thinking is often used in academic and business worlds. It is about focusing on the problem. It is about analysing the problem in detail to find a solution. It is logical and linear. It is about why, what, when... where, which...

Creative Thinking

Creative thinking is often described as thinking *out* of the box.
In everyday life creative thinking is thinking about what can be done *with the box* itself.
It involves thinking about creating new prospects with the same circumstances...
as in everyday life it is a bit like people to change all their circumstances at once.
It is thinking about the 'how'...

In daily life too much critical thinking can keep one focused on the problem for too long. It is better to apply creative thinking instead. Instead of thinking why something does not work, it may be better to think about 'how' something could work.
Change 'why' questions to 'how' questions.

We can't solve problems by using the same kind of thinking we used when we created them.
Albert Einstein

Do: Select a routine task that feels like a chore and try to look at it completely differently, apply creativity to it. How could you do it differently?

Daydreaming

Daydreaming is imagining beautiful and wonderful things.
It's imagining that you are very rich or very famous.
It is fantasizing about things that are possibly not real.
Daydreaming is often a form of escapism.
At times it is about avoiding reality.

Visualization

Visualization is creating a mental picture of the things that we want to achieve.
It is about imagining achieving our Goal.
Visualization is not just about the goal itself but about the process as well.
It is about creating a mental image of actually doing the things that are needed in order to get to your goal.

Daydreaming is a waste of time.
Instead try to visualize your best possible self – doing and being your best.
Use visualization to create action towards your goals.

Visualization is when your dreams have a real purpose.

Exercise: Find some alone time. Close your eyes and visualize your best possible self. How would you be? What would you be doing? What would your ideal life look like? Do this for no more than 15 minutes, then write down three small new things that you can start applying to your present life right now.

Benefit

Benefit is something we gain. It is what we get at the end of a process, activity or involvement.

Example: When we go on a holiday, we benefit from the stimulation and inspiration we get from the change of scenery… new place, different food… different language.

Reason

Reason is why we do things in the first place. It is slightly different from the actual benefit that we get in the end.

If you are constantly yearning and pining to go away from your daily life all the time, examine, what is the reason? Is it perhaps boredom and dissatisfaction with your current life and with what you are doing on a daily basis? Examine your real reasons for doing things.

Try to find the reason why you do things and don't just focus on the benefit.

If your reason to do something or not to do something aligns with who you are… the benefit will automatically be valuable to your life.

Focus also on the reason and not just the benefit.

If reasons are good, the benefits that follow will also be good.

Think about: A recent activity or social event that you joined or attended. Think about the outcome and benefits; also think about the deeper reasons you got involved…

Roadblocks

When one thing doesn't go exactly the way we want it to go... we get bogged down with the negativity of the situation and then often other things also start to appear like obstacles. Everything piles up...
When we start to see difficult situations as obstacles they become roadblocks.

Bridges

Challenging situations can provide opportunity. A possibility to do something new. Whenever something does not go the way we want, it's an opportunity for something new to happen. Something we did not anticipate might work out better than what we had imagined.
When we start to see difficult situations as opportunities they turn into bridges.

Create an attitude of seeing opportunity and not just seeing problems.

If you want opportunity you have to focus on what's possible and not just the problems.
Opportunities are the bridges that connect us to new things.
Construct bridges and don't create internal roadblocks.

Idea: With friends, brainstorm ideas regarding a challenging situation. Pay attention to how they see the problem. Note where the problem turns into a bridge and where it becomes a roadblock.

Struggling

There are so many things going on at the same time in our lives. Work commitments, family obligations, health stuff, home decoration, holiday plans, birthdays, anniversaries etc. Sometimes with many things going on all together it seems near impossible to manage everything at the same time. Things then start slipping and then this creates more and more stress.
Struggling is not fun.

Juggling

Juggling is the art of keeping several objects in the air without dropping them. Skilled Jugglers can keep many balls in the air at the same time.
How can they achieve this?
It is achieved by keeping the eye on one ball at a time and coordinating and balancing others.
Every Juggler knows how many balls they are able to keep in the air at the same time and how many balls are too much.
Jugglers enjoy juggling.

Don't struggle with everything at the same time.
Know your number – how many balls can you successfully keep in the air at the same time?
Decide that you will no longer struggle; juggle instead.
Enjoy juggling.

Give up struggling, start Juggling and enjoy it!

Try this: Make a to-do monthly list. Organize the tasks and chores across four weeks. Don't try to squeeze all the boring stuff together; sandwich it in between other interesting stuff and juggle it well!

Outcome

Outcome is how things turn out, it's the result of something. At times we get so caught up in solely focusing on the outcome, we lose sight of what is happening now.
We forget the present and get anxious about what may or may not happen in the future.

Process

Process is the method we use in order to achieve the outcome we want.
Process is what is happening now.
Process is the journey.

Focus more on the process. This will release the anxiety about the outcome and about the future.
If you enjoy the process, whatever the outcome it'll be worth it.

Striving for something better in the future is fine as long as we are fully aware and appreciative of what is happening now.

Think about: A task or project whose outcome you are worried about. Turn your attention towards the process. Think about how you could enjoy the process more.

Fixed Mindset

Someone who has a fixed mindset believes that our intelligence and talents are fixed and cannot be enhanced. To them what we are born with is more vital than what we can learn.

People with a fixed mindset are afraid to do new things, as they fear failure. They are afraid to make any sorts of mistakes as they feel they won't be able to rectify them.

Growth Mindset

People with a growth mindset believe in effort. They believe that with effort things can be learned and developed.

People with a growth mindset learn from mistakes. They are not afraid of failure; they see it as an opportunity to make themselves better.

With a growth mindset people grow and develop; with a fixed mindset people remain fixed.

Exam results just show the current state of the individual; they don't guarantee anything about the future. Success does not come from Talent itself, it comes from effort.

Question: Are you a person with a Fixed mindset or a Growth mindset?

Post-Traumatic Stress

When something really bad happens, we experience stress as the aftermath of the trauma.
Post-traumatic stress causes feelings of distress and anxiety. There is enough understanding of how this stress negatively affects us. There are also enough interventions for reducing this stress.
We know that trauma brings us stress and suffering, but perhaps there is also the other side to this coin?

Post-Traumatic Growth

When we experience something bad or traumatic, it is important to remember that life brings a variety of experiences to us. And these experiences teach us something new... and this learning can enable growth within us.
Once the traumatic experience has passed and the dust has settled, it is also a good idea to reflect on the lessons learned and insights gained alongside the suffering.
Suffering from trauma may indeed be present but perhaps there is also some increased sense of strength, meaning, understanding... This is the other side of the coin.

I lost everything in the flood. It took my house and all my things.
First I was very angry and very upset but after a while...
I am so grateful that my family was all fine.
I may have lost my possessions, but I regained my family. Now I don't collect 'things', I collect moments.
Anonymous

That which does not kill us, makes us stronger.
Friedrich Nietzsche

Suggestion: Find a person you respect. Ask them if they can think of a past experience that was traumatic and find out what positive insights they gained as a result of that experience.

Why?

It is good to be aware of our own true reason behind doing something, but at times 'Why' can become a defence mechanism to keep us in the familiar territory. Sometimes whenever something new scares us, 'Why' becomes more like finding an excuse for 'not doing' something...

When starting new activities, new hobbies and learning new things scares us, we automatically start an internal dialogue... Why waste energy? Why would this help me? Why is this necessary? Why create more stress for something new? This type of internal reasoning is more about the internal mechanism that keeps us stuck in our comfort zone rather than exploring the true reasons for doing or not doing something.

Why not!

Why not! is about moving away from the internal stuck position that negatively justifies that 'not doing' something is correct, even when in our heart we know we really like to do it. It's about saying to yourself, 'I like salsa dancing... maybe I can take some classes to learn it, well why not!'

Why not! Is not a question but it is a self-expression that propels action.

Next time you are hesitating to do something that you know deep inside is good for you... but the fear of the new is stopping you, just say to yourself – Why Not!

When you are hesitating about something new, that you know could be good...
change your internal dialogue from Why? to Why not!

I hear you say, 'Why?' Always 'Why?' You see things; and you say, 'Why?' But I dream things that never were; and I say, 'Why not.'
George Bernard Shaw

Try this: Think of a new thing that you would like to learn.
Just say to yourself firmly – Why Not!
How does that feel?

Trait

Traits are some characteristics about us that don't change much over time.
They can be physical, for example height, skin colour, colour of eyes...
They can also be about the personality, like some people are 'artistic', some are 'sporty', some are 'musical' etc., etc...
Traits remain somewhat the same over time.

State

State is the mood we are in at the present moment.
We could be feeling anxious, nervous, stressed, happy, sad etc.
We can influence our state by creating awareness of the present moment.
By creating awareness of how we are in the present moment, we can influence our state to become more positive.

Being in a positive state is very important as it is the key to how we interact with the world around us, regardless of our traits.

If we keep our present state pleasant, our traits will have the best opportunity to shine.

Question: How are you really feeling right now? Become aware of your present state and describe your present feelings in detail.

Equal

Equal means exact.
Equal means everyone gets 'exactly the same', regardless of their efforts or needs.
A small piece of bread may be sufficient for a two-year-old toddler but it won't be enough for a teenager. It may be equal in quantity but is not equivalent to their need.
Equality is about mathematics.

Fair

Fair is about correctness and not about mathematics.
Fair does not mean everyone gets exactly the same; it means everyone gets what they deserve according to their needs or efforts.

Fair isn't always equal.
Fair is ensuring that everyone receives what he or she needs or deserves.

Equality is just calculation. Fairness is correctness.

Suggestion: Notice if anyone around you is being treated unfairly. What could you do to help correct that?

Rigidity

Rigidity means to be strong and tough. It means not to bend. In life it means having one fixed idea about what should happen and sticking to it… and when things don't turn out the exact way, one cannot see a way forward at all. Rigidity is not really a strength but a weakness.

Resilience

Resilience does not only mean being strong and tough, but also having the capacity for change and adaptability. It means when circumstances are tough, one has the strength to stand the blows and bounce back rather than be broken. Resilience in life means having the strength to cope when something bad happens or things don't go the way we want them to go. It means having the ability to cope with change and the courage to see a way forward.

The main difference between rigidity and resilience is the ability to withstand the stress and strains of life and have the ability to bounce back and keep moving.

The green reed which bends in the wind is stronger than the mighty oak which breaks in a storm.
Chinese proverb

Think of: Past events in your life that seemed like disastrous blows at the time but you successfully bounced backed and moved forward… reflect on your inner resilience.

Detach

Detachment is a buzzword in the spiritual world but perhaps at times in everyday life it can be misunderstood. It can often be misinterpreted as – staying at a safe distance from everyone or not being involved on a personal level with anything or anyone. Sometimes people become disinterested in others and think that perhaps that is the way to remain 'detached'. They stop caring and become emotionless. This is not detachment.
Detachment can be a complex thing to fully understand and follow in everyday life.

Disentangle

Be caring towards others, be interested in others and be genuinely concerned about their needs. However, it is a good idea not to get tangled up in their dramas.
Care and genuine concern is good as long as someone else's problems do not entangle our own sense of well-being or perceptiveness.
Remaining disentangled is as good as detachment.

Detachment is a virtue, however, at times it is difficult to grasp exactly what detachment means in everyday life. Involvement is a necessary part of living a full life. Being 'disconnected' from living and feeling is not real detachment.
It is a lifelong practice to become fully detached.
Perhaps an easier way to follow it is to substitute it with disentanglement.
If you feel that you are being disturbed with someone else's problems so much that you yourself need help, then it's a good idea to step back a bit.

Don't worry about getting 'detachment' right, just try not to get so tangled up in others' dramas that you lose your own sense of well-being or perspective.

Idea: Next time a friend or a relative is talking about their problems, observe yourself. How are you being affected? Are you able to stay detached/disentangled yet concerned and caring towards them?

Black and White

Black and white is about extremes. It is about all or nothing. Often in life things evolve at their own pace and in the middle there are all sorts of variations.
A successful businessman may appear to have it all now, but in the middle stages it wasn't so black and white for him either. There were perhaps some failures along the way.
Success and failure are not black and white. Failure can have some elements of success in the making.
What may appear a failure to you now is perhaps success in disguise...

Shades of Grey

Shades of grey means there are variations in life.
What others have or have achieved is their reality not yours.
In our own journey we are evolving and have our own variety of experiences.
Someone's failure is another one's success.
Between black and white the shades vary for everyone.

Success and failure are not black or white.
In life there are shades of greys.
Your shade of grey is your own variation.
Don't compare it with the white of others.

Don't define your world in black and white, because there is so much hiding amongst the greys.
Unknown

Think about: Something that seemed a failure for you at the time but in hindsight actually turned out to be an opportunity for something else...

Rock Bottom

Once in our life we may hit rock bottom. When everything seems bleak. It feels like the worst place to be. It feels like everything will continue going down forever. It feels like nothing will ever get better.
It is the feeling of total despair and everything seems impossible. There seems to be nothing going on that feels positive. It feels like being in the lowest place ever.
It feels like rock bottom.

Solid Foundation

When you feel you are at the lowest point possible ever, think of it as not the worst place but the first place to be. When you are at your lowest you can start to build a strong solid foundation there.
The foundations of tall buildings are at their very lowest level.
Imagine a building with a poor and unstable foundation. In the future this building will perhaps not be strong enough to withstand the storms.
So, since you are already at your lowest point here's your chance to get started on building that solid foundation.

Being at the lowest is not a calamity; it is actually a chance to construct a solid foundation.
Some buildings are built tall but their foundation is not strong.
When you are at rock bottom rebuild a solid foundation for the future.

Rock bottom became solid foundation on which I rebuilt my life.
JK Rowling

Think about: A time in your life when you felt like rock bottom. What actions could you take now in order not to feel like that again?

Habits

Habit is something we do automatically without awareness.
We all have some good habits and some not so good habits.
At times it can be challenging to get rid of some bad habits and likewise it can be also quite difficult to form new good habits.

Regular Activities

Regular activities are some things we do often.
Like watching our favourite TV show, eating pizza on Friday night, talking about X whenever Y calls…
It is important to be aware of your regular activities as they will soon turn into habits.

When we want to create a new habit, it is easier to think of it in terms of just an activity.
Rather than pressure yourself, 'I must get into the habit of going to the gym', just diarize to play badminton three times a week…
Things done regularly become your habits.
Our habits and activities ultimately become our life.

Keep your habits positive because your habits become your values. Keep your values positive because your values become your destiny.
Mahatma Gandhi

Try this: Check your regular activities. Which ones are turning into your habits?

Copy

A copy is a replica of something. An identical duplicate.
Sometimes in life you may get a bit impressed with the lives of others. You want what they have… a car same as theirs, a big house same as theirs, a lifestyle same as theirs.
Some people post photos of holidays and parties on Facebook in order to appear just like others…
Why would you want to be exactly the same as others?
Why would you want to be a copy?

Original

Originality is about uniqueness. In reality no matter how much we may want to be like others, we are all unique and original. Not even identical twins are exactly the same.
Be proud of who you are, embrace your originality. Don't chase a lifestyle or concepts of happiness that work for others. Create your own.
You are not a copy, you are original.

It seems that the idea of a good life is the same photocopy floating around the entire world.
We are all trying so hard to have the same life. A big house, a big car, fame, parties…
Have we all lost our own original print?

Everyone is original. Why try so hard to become a copy! Embrace your originality.

Think about: Your best friend. What is original and unique about his/her way of being?

Reducing Weaknesses

When you are not good at something and you keep focusing on it you are likely to feel even worse about it.
Why not focus on a strength instead of what you are not good at?
For example: Someone is not good at socializing at parties or bars and does not meet new people that way. Their strength is creativity. They can focus on their strength and enhance it further by joining a creative class (sculpturing/drawing/painting) and meet new people there.
Instead of forcing themselves to socialize at parties or bars with strangers, which is not their strength, they use the strength that they do have to enhance other areas of their life.

Building Strengths

Building strengths is about identifying your internal qualities and then using them in everyday life to enhance them further.
Our inner character strengths not only help us to deal with problems in life, they also help us to experience more joy and fulfilment.
Some strengths are:
Forgiveness, Bravery, Humility, Creativity, Prudence, Leadership, Self-Regulation, Teamwork, Kindness, Persistence, Honesty, Social Intelligence… and many more…

Inner character strengths are virtues in action.
Knowing and using your virtues has a positive impact on your life.
Positive psychology research has shown that when we effectively apply our strengths, they are beneficial not only to us but also to people around us and society as a whole.

The good life is using your signature strengths every day to produce authentic happiness and abundant gratification.
Martin Seligman

Exercise: Write down three strengths you have. For each strength write an activity or action to enhance it further.
Example: Strength is kindness – Today while driving I will give way to others.

Perfection

Perfection is about our own perception rather than the situation or the person.
Some of us are hung up on perfection.
We want things to be perfect but a perfect job or a perfect relationship actually means different things to different people.
Sometimes our internal need for perfection can stagnate us.
We either sit around waiting for the perfect partner, situation or job to appear or we remain dissatisfied with what we have.

Accomplishment

Accomplishment is about achieving something.
Are you able to achieve harmony and love in a relationship?
Are you able to reach job satisfaction in your current job?
Accomplishing something is about progress in the right direction; the need for perfection can sometimes hinder that progress.

Keep your focus on accomplishing something rather than making it perfect.

Perfection can sometimes stagnate us.
Not being hung up on perfection does not mean letting go of your standards...
It just means allowing yourself the approval to move forward.

Think about: One thing/project that you have not been able to complete for a long time... What is the real reason for its stagnation? Is it perfection?

Entitlement Mentality

Entitlement mentality is when someone thinks that they are owed something from others.
Society owes them a living.
Partner owes them respect.
Children owe them gratitude.
They think to claim from others is their right. They take others for granted.
They expect to be treated as a priority in situations for no apparent reason.

Merit Mentality

Merit mentality is when someone knows that no one owes them anything.
Whatever one deserves is based on one's own merit.
They earn a living through effort.
They gain respect through their character.
They cultivate gratitude though their own practice.
They don't think that others should automatically give them importance.
They don't take others for granted and they appreciate and value others.

People with entitlement mentality assume that privileges should come to them automatically.
People with merit mentality know that nothing comes automatically.
Everything is earned with effort.

Entitlement mentality destroys societies and damages relationships.

Do: Make a list of things or people you take for granted. Convert that list into a gratitude list.

Finite

We are aware of things that have a definable limit. We hold on to these closely as we feel they might finish or run out someday.
At times we hold on to these a bit too cautiously... our money, our time, fuel, chocolate, wine... we share them sparingly.

Infinite

It is good to remember we also have some things that don't finish.
They are boundless, limitless, abundant...
We can share them and use them as much as possible...
They won't finish.
Love, compassion, laughter, gratitude, empathy, kindness, smiles, hugs, kisses...

Whilst counting the finite, don't forget the power of the infinite. The abundance that lies within – love, joy, compassion, gratitude...

Chocolate and wine may run out, but Hugs and Kisses won't. Hugs and Kisses are calorie-free, relieve sadness and can be shared as much as possible.

Suggestion: Give a surprise visit to a friend and give them a generous hug and a kiss on the cheek... you can also take along some chocolates.

Get Rid of Bad Things

Pesticide kills germs. It gets rid of the bugs that destroy the plant.
Do you live only by solving problems?
Do you just focus on what needs to be resolved, rectified and remedied?
Are you a perpetual bug killer?

Grow Good Things

Fertilizer is a substance added to the soil to make plants grow well.
It is a good idea to do things that enhance the positive things in your life and not just concentrate on getting rid of the problems.
Add fertilizer regularly to grow good things.

Don't just concentrate on getting rid of the negative stuff.
Also do stuff regularly that makes you happy.
Getting rid of the bugs is good, but you also have to keep planting new seeds.

You cannot collect darkness and throw it out.
In order to remove darkness one has to produce light.
Go produce light.

Suggestion: Celebrate something. Think of a special day, a birthday of a friend, an anniversary of a relative, promotion of a friend… arrange an event to celebrate together with them.

Rationalisation

Rationalisation is about coming up with logical reasoning. When something happens we try to rationalise it in our heads. We analyse it, dissect it, scrutinize it and try to find logical reasons to fix it. In an attempt to get it back to exactly what it was like before.
Like when a vase breaks we pick up the pieces and try very hard to meticulously glue them back together just how it was. You may be able to glue it back together with great effort but the cracks will always remain.

Redesign

Redesigning is when we try to create something completely different with what was.
We use what has happened, but we don't just apply reasoning to it. We apply creativity and come up with something new. When a vase breaks we can use the broken pieces not to glue it back together to the way it was, but to create something new. We can make a mosaic or a wall decoration with the pieces instead of trying to reconstruct the same vase again.

Don't just rationalise.
Use creativity, don't be afraid to use your spontaneous imagination.
Create something new.
If a relationship breaks down, perhaps it will never be the same again, but maybe it can mean something new?

The intuitive mind is a sacred gift and the rational mind is a faithful servant.
We have created a society that honours the servant and has forgotten the gift.
Albert Einstein

Think about: What areas of your life have changed that you are not quite satisfied with. How could you redesign them?
For example: Some time ago you were a fitness fanatic, you

vigorously jogged every day for one hour but because of your knee problem you can no longer do that... What could you do differently now to get fit? Take up a light yoga class? Do occasional salsa dancing?

Mind-glasses

Mind-glasses have mental lenses through which we see things.

Our mental lenses have various filters.

These filters can be our beliefs, attitudes, prejudices, language, bias, viewpoints, and experiences...

Some of these filters can sometimes make us see things in a distorted way.

Worst-case scenarios – I'll be homeless.

Overgeneralizations – All my colleagues are better at everything.

Comparisons – She is a better mum than me.

Assumptions – I did not reply to his email and now he hates me.

I-glasses

Eyeglasses make our vision accurate. Through them we see things as they are and not according to our sight. They correct our poor vision.

Perhaps, when we distort things in our head, we need to apply I-glass vision instead of mind-glass vision.

Ask yourself some clarity questions:

Worst-case scenarios – What is realistically likely to happen?

Overgeneralizations – How do I know that?

Comparisons – In which way exactly?

Assumptions – What specifically makes me think that?

Mind has many filters. Filters can sometimes distort our mind vision.

The important thing is to become aware of these filters.

Mind-glasses can get out of focus at times. We start to see things in a distorted way.

Swap the mind-glasses for your I-glasses to see correctly.

By simply applying some clarity questions they reduce conditions of exaggeration, overgeneralizations and assumptions.

Do: Use your I-glasses, apply some clarity questions… you will start seeing your exaggerations, overgeneralizations, assumptions…

Being Understood

When we say things like:
She does not understand me.
He did not get me.
No one understands me.
They didn't understand what I said.what is being understood about her, him and them?

Explaining

Being fully understood by someone is about 'your ability' not theirs.
It is about how well you explain what you need to convey to others.
It is about explaining the message according to the other person's understanding.
Do you gear your message according to the audience or according to just what makes sense to you?
Example: If you are explaining something to five-year-olds you will automatically use the words and language that will make sense to them.

Being understood is your responsibility and not the responsibility of the other person.
It is about your ability to explain what you need to convey to others.
When someone misunderstands you, don't be offended.
It is just missed-understanding not misunderstanding.
Explain again.

No one will come along one fine day and understand you and everything about you completely just the way you want them to. It will only happen when you have actually acquired the ability to explain yourself clearly to them.

Exercise: Next time you have to explain something complex to someone think about them first and not the message. Think about what and how you need to say according to their understanding and not just yours.

Unlucky

Do you believe in luck?
If something bad happens is it because of bad luck?
If a robber shoots you in the arm, grabs your wallet and runs away –
Do you think you are unlucky?

Lucky

Good luck is about changing the perception of things in a positive way. It is also about positively accepting the things that cannot be changed.
If a robber shoots you in the arm, grabs your wallet and runs away –
Do you consider yourself lucky?

You may think luck is something external, something outside your control.
Actually, luck is a matter of your own perception.
If you perceive yourself to be lucky, you will often find yourself good luck.
Cultivate a luck mindset. Notice and create lucky opportunities.

The day you decide to do it is your lucky day.
Japanese proverb

Exercise: Find some good luck today. Go on be lucky!

Lie Factory

Sometimes the Lie Factory inside the mind goes into overproduction.
I am no good. I am not worth it. It'll never happen. I don't know enough. I am not cool… I am not OK… I can't get anything right, I am a loser…
It keeps on churning such lies…

Contentment Works

When the Lie Factory goes into overproduction it's best to commission Contentment Works to take over the production plant. It can start producing positive thoughts.
I am full of positive energy. I am capable of trying. I have my own strengths. I can learn new things. I am OK… I have been successful with various things in the past, I can do it again…

What's inside your head, Lie Factory or Contentment Works?

The worst lies are the lies we tell ourselves.
We live in denial of what we do, even what we think.
We do this because we're afraid. We fear we will not find love,
and when we find it we fear we'll lose it.
We fear that if we don't have love we will be unhappy.
Richard Bach

Suggestion: Try to become aware when your Lie Factory goes into overproduction…

Simplification

Everyone wants a simple life.
What is a simple life?
A simple life is a life without complications, difficulties, problems...
How does one get rid of all the complications, difficulties, problems from their entire life?
Is that even possible?
It appears that to make one's life simple is actually a very complicated thing.

Subtraction

Subtraction is a simple act of deduction.
Just remove some things from your life.
- Instead of 5 meals a day, have 3.
- If there are 15 things to do on your 'to-do list', delete 4. Just decide which 4 things you don't need to do at all.
- If you have 30 pairs of shoes, get rid of the 5 you haven't used in last three months.

Subtraction is simple.

Instead of trying to get your head around simplification, just subtract.
Subtraction is much easier and life will automatically become simpler.
Just reduce, deduct, subtract, minus, get rid of... let go of...

Knowledge is learning something every day.
Wisdom is letting go of something every day.
Zen Proverb

Think about: Which three things or useless ways of thinking you can subtract from your life right now?

Certainty

We all want certainty. We want to know what will happen next. In reality certainty does not exist.
We can't predict anything with absolute certainty.
We can plan well, but we cannot predict with 100% certainty what will exactly happen next.
When things don't happen exactly according to our expectation, we get disappointed, hurt and sometimes experience pain and loss of motivation.

Clarity

Clarity is a sense of knowing. Knowing about the purpose not the outcome.
Having clarity about something is the deep understanding of 'why' we do something.
It's a feeling, not an expectation.
It is a deep understanding that comes from within.
It's a way of thinking.
'I don't know exactly what will happen in the end, but I am sure about this now... I am clear about it.'

Instead of striving for certainty aim to develop clarity.
Be clear about your motives.
What are you doing now... and why are you doing it?

Nothing is ever certain, but something should remain clear.
Seek clarity and not certainty.

Do: List three things in your life that are not certain, but which you are absolutely clear about.

Controlling

We are all a little bit of control junkies. We want things to happen in our own way. We want predictable outcomes, we want people to say and do what we want... and when this does not happen we feel disappointed.

Trusting

Trusting is allowing things to evolve in their own way and being OK with unexpected outcome. This does not mean completely letting go of everything and not making any plans; it just means remaining positive and confident about situations and people.

We cannot control anyone or any situation but we can trust people and situations.

Trusting is far more powerful than controlling.

Trust the journey, don't try to control it. It will be more enjoyable then.

Trust me!

Think about: Who and what do you trust completely?

Love Hurts

If love was such a wonderful thing then why would it hurt? We use terms such as 'fallen in love', 'blind in love', 'crazy in love'…

If love really makes us fall and then we get hurt and we also become blind and crazy, then love does not sound like such a great thing at all! Does it?!

Love Heals

Love does not hurt but it heals.

Love is actually the cure for pain and hurt.

Love is the medicine for the soul.

To give love and receive love is the most meaningful experience we can have in our lives.

Love is what gives us meaning.

If love makes us fall, it makes us blind, crazy and it hurts… then why is the entire world seeking love!

***We need to change our notions about love.
It does not hurt us or make us blind. We do not fall in love.
We become aware in love. We rise in love, we heal with love.
When we see love differently, we will know its true worth.***

Think about: A time when you felt hurt 'because of love'… was the pain really because of love or because of something else? Was it because of your own expectations, your own interpretations… something else?

Self-Awareness

Human Doing

We get caught up in do, do, do... We are doing, doing all the time...
This is OK, as we all have to do daily chores and tasks that we cannot neglect.
There is nothing wrong with doing as doing is necessary.
It is good to be active, but quite often we are doing without thought.
It's as if we are almost not alive.
We are rushing here and there on autopilot.
It's like we are following a preprogrammed routine.
We are 'doing' like we are machines, like robots.

Human Being

'Being' does not mean not doing anything. Being means to do things consciously.
It means to be aware of what's happening around you in the moment.
Being also means allowing things to happen without the need to control...
No matter how much you try, you cannot 'do' control, you can only 'be' in control.
Human being means to let go of the fear with which we do the stuff.
It means to be present in the moment fully and not let the fear about the next moment interfere with what's happening now. Just be.

Ask yourself, 'Do I get caught up in do, do, do...?'
Learn to create the right positive balance between doing and being.
We are alive foremost because of our being; then after that we think, feel, reason and do.

You are a human being, not a human doing.
Learn to be first, then to do.

Suggestion: Observe yourself during the day. What does ideal balance between doing and being look like? Are you active/receptive; restless/patient; talking/listening; reacting/insightful...

Living to Eat

Food is necessary for survival.
It is a main motivational factor for all living creatures.
However, we humans, we no longer see food as a motivational factor for our lives.
As we don't need to go and find it every day in order to survive.
For us food is so readily and easily available everywhere (in most parts of the world) that we have learned to eat for pleasure rather than to stay alive.
If we don't like the taste of something it gives us no pleasure and we discard it easily. We have plenty to choose from.
We think food is there for our enjoyment.
Food to us is now a form of an entertainment rather than a necessity.

Eating to Live

Too much importance is now placed on 'pleasure' in relation to food.
We eat for the pleasure of it.
We focus far too much on the taste rather than nutrition. This is fine, but we also do need to remember that food is our nutrition.
We eat so that we can stay alive.
Perhaps, we need to rebalance our relationship with food and not take it for granted or just see it as an entertainment.

In relation to food, perhaps we now need to focus a little bit more on nutrition and a little less on pleasure alone.

Choose better so you can love food more.
Be grateful for the food you eat.
It gives you life not just pleasure.

Exercise: Prepare and eat two meals a week with your focus solely on nutrition and not on taste. Before you start your meal, tell yourself that you will enjoy every mouthful as it is a blessing.

Childlike

In fashion magazines most models look childlike. They are all slim and slender, and they have beautiful, flawless glowing complexions, just like children.

Somewhere along the line in our quest for beauty we have perhaps got a bit confused.

For a grown woman to appear childlike is considered a sign of beauty.

In order to retain the external everlasting childlike appearance, are we are also retaining childishness?

Isn't it a bit childish to desire to look as if your age and years have not progressed?

Youthful

Youthfulness is different from being childlike. It is not about the external appearance; it's about inner joy and playfulness. Being youthful means remaining light-hearted and enthusiastic.

It means remaining open to discovering new things and having the capacity to enjoy the little things of everyday life.

Being youthful does not mean acting without responsibility. It means having the ability to remain light even in the face of adversity. It means with passing time and years your inner joy still remains intact.

Get rid of your childishness, but no matter how old you get retain youthfulness.

A true joyous heartfelt laughter can make you appear youthful in more ways than any face cream or make-up ever can.

Youth is happy because it has the capacity to see beauty. Anyone who keeps the ability to see beauty never grows old.
Franz Kafka

Try this: Find the funny side of everyday mundane situations and balance it between taking things seriously and not taking them too seriously.

Ideal Self

Our ideal self is an image in our mind of how we want to be. The way we want to look, the way we want to behave and the way we want to be living our life.

Often there is some discrepancy in how we actually are and how we want to be.

It is OK to want to be slightly different from our real self, to develop and grow, but when we keep fantasizing about being completely different we become deeply unhappy.

Real Self

Our real self is who we are in our daily life. It is how we actually look, think, feel and behave.

We need to know our real self really well. Knowing and being our real self does not mean we cannot aspire for change and development. When we know our real self well we can improve things about ourselves. We can acquire more strength, more patience, more courage, more determination... learn new things and improve our health and well-being.

The first step towards any improvement is awareness and love for your real self.

Love your real self and at the same time keep working on creating your ideal self.

The privilege of a lifetime is to become who you truly are.

CG Jung

Exercise: On a sheet of paper make two columns. List your Real-self qualities and your Ideal-self qualities.

Style

Style is mostly about appearance, how something or someone looks.
Someone can look sophisticated, elegant, fashionable or trendy… it is mainly about the external presentation.
Sometimes a lot of importance is placed on how things are presented or how someone looks.
Everyone wants to look impressive.

Substance

Substance is about the content, how valuable something is.
Popularity, fame, status… are all about style.
Truth, honour, reliability, integrity… are about the actual substance.

We are perhaps getting too concerned with how many likes we get on our Facebook photo rather than how many real people we actually get on well with in real life.

Instead of worrying about, 'How do I look to others?' Isn't it better to ask yourself, 'Who am I as a person?'

Exercise: Next time you go out for a social event don't just think about what you will wear; think about how you will be with other people… friendly, caring, interested, approachable, welcoming, kind, sympathetic, helpful, attentive…

Boring

Something uninteresting is boring.
In the present world sensationalism stands out.
When something is extreme, it is considered thrilling.
Something stable and steady is considered boring.
Boring means not finding anything interesting or motivating in anything.
If you can't find anything interesting about something, how are you looking at it?
Often boring comes from within.
Bored people are boring.

Balanced

Balance does not mean an artificial state of perpetual equanimity where nothing can imbalance the state ever.
Sometimes most of us get angry, shout, have bad moods, cry, feel sad, feel excited...
Balance means creating the right stability by putting the right weights on either side.
In life, this means understanding that happiness alone does not create equilibrium.
It is knowing that happiness and sorrow are both needed to balance the scales.
If one does not experience sorrow at all, how will one know what happiness is?
Being balanced is not boring.

Creating the right positive balance is perhaps the ultimate art and pursuits of this life.

Understanding balance is important.
It is knowing that happiness alone cannot create equilibrium as it can only be known and felt in relation to sorrow.

Think about: A person in your life you consider well balanced. Think about how they are, how they deal with things in their life that makes them well balanced.

Lonely	Alone
Lonely is an emotional state.	Alone is a physical state. Alone is when one is physically by themselves.
Lonely means not feeling happy to be by yourself.	Being alone does not mean one is unhappy to be by themselves.
One can be lonely even in a crowd.	Being alone is being in solitude; it does not mean emotional isolation.
Lonely is when one is not able to connect with others and feels emotionally isolated.	Although prolonged social isolation is sometimes not good, solitude and silence can stimulate creativity and create peace.
Feeling lonely all the time is not good.	

It is good to be alone sometimes but it is not good to feel lonely. Cultivate the habit to spend some time alone daily but when you feel lonely connect with friends and family.

Loneliness does not come from having no people about, but from being unable to communicate the things that seem important to oneself.
CG Jung

Try this: Spend time alone regularly. Meditate or read something interesting. Enjoy being alone.

Passive Victim

Accepting negative situations in life without doing anything to change the situation and then wallowing in self-pity is being a passive victim.

A passive victim blames circumstances and people. He/she believes that someone else or outside circumstances are responsible for their well-being and they themselves cannot do anything about it.

Active Agent

An active agent proactively engages with the situation, takes responsibility and does not blame circumstances or people.

An active agent knows that although not everything can be controlled, there are things that can be done to create positive change in one's own life.

Be an active agent.
Active agents look at themselves before they point a finger at someone else.

Observe yourself in those difficult situations.
Are you being a passive victim or an active agent?

Suggestion: Next time something happens that makes you think 'poor me', 'why me', write down three actions that will improve the situation and your feeling. Carry them out.

Ego

Ego is about self-importance and it needs validation and approval from others. It likes competition and thinks it is better than others.
Ego is an attachment to the image of the self in a way that it gets easily hurt when others don't do what it wants or say what it wants to hear.
It uses various defence mechanisms to protect itself.
Ego relies on position, power, wealth, status, appearance and all external things... and when these go away, it feels it has nothing and feels lost...

Self Esteem

Self-esteem is a deep sense of self-worth.
It is not about feeling important but about knowing that you are valuable.
Self-esteem means liking yourself and respecting yourself.
Validation and approval come from within and are not based on external factors.
Self-esteem is not dependent on what others think and it does not need to be defended.
Self-esteem does not take offence and accepts criticism constructively.
Self-esteem is based on virtues such as self-respect, compassion, determination... and these cannot be lost or taken away by someone else.

We all have an ego.
It is good to beware when our ego kicks into action.
It is good to speak out our opinions but not to the extent that we become defensive about them.
When we overly defend our opinion, it becomes more about our ego's need to be right than the topic.
Nurture your self-esteem by choosing to remain positive about yourself regardless of others' approval of your opinions.
Maintain a healthy sense of self and learn to take valid criticism and not feel wounded by it.

Look after your self-esteem; not your ego!

Suggestion: Discuss a topic important to you with your friends. Observe yourself during the conversation. Are you defending your ego or just presenting your opinion?

Success

What does being successful mean?
Material things in everyday conversation often define success.
Someone who is considered successful has a lucrative business, big house, flashy car, six-figure salary, goes on exotic holidays etc., etc.
We all want to be successful in life.
Being successful projects an appearance of a fulfilled life.
But we also know about some of those successful famous musicians, actors, sports people, businessmen who have all of the above but are far from leading a fulfilled life.

Fulfilment

Fulfilment is a feeling that comes from feeling satisfied and complete regardless of material possessions, career achievements or status quo.
There are lists of Top 100 successful businesspeople in the world, or Top 100 richest, actors, musicians etc...
Perhaps as fulfilment cannot be judged from the outside there are no lists of Top 100 most fulfilled people in the world.
It is often believed fulfilment follows success. When one is successful, there will be that inner feeling of fulfilment.
However, this is not true. Quite often successful people remain unfulfilled.
Fulfilment is a feeling of being content with what you have in the moment. It has little to do with possessions, or external portrayal of worldly success.

It is good to aim to achieve our goals but it is very important to remember that fulfilment is not dependent on success.
Fulfilment lies within.
Fulfilment makes us happy. Success makes us proud.
It is good to feel fulfilment in the present moment...
Rather than wait for it to happen one fine day in the future.

Fulfilment is created and felt from within; success is external. No matter how successful one may be externally, this does not guarantee inner fulfilment.

Idea: Create a (mental or physical) storyboard of your life so far. Your successes and your learnings. Generate a feeling of fulfilment. Feel everything is as it should be and that you are satisfied and fulfilled with what has been and whatever is happening right now.

Self-sabotage

Self-sabotage is when we keep telling ourselves off.
It is indulging in self-blame.
We keep reminding ourselves what we are lacking, what we have done wrong and what we are not capable of.
We keep hindering our own progress by our own negative self-beliefs.
Self-sabotage is like a virus that stops the computer from functioning properly.

Self-sovereignty

Sovereignty means to have power, control and independence.
It does not mean never to take instructions from someone else.
We all have authority figures such as bosses, teachers, parents etc. around us and they give us instructions or guidance from time to time, and it is absolutely fine to follow that.
Self-sovereignty just means freedom from our own internal negative beliefs.
To have the power to rise above our own internal negative self-sabotaging thoughts.

Watch how you self-sabotage.
'I never get anything right.'
'I cannot make friends.'
Have sovereignty over yourself, change these negative thoughts to –
'I may get things wrong sometimes but I also get some things right at other times and I am capable of learning from my mistakes.'
'I do have some friends and I am developing the art of making new friends.'

In order to be a true sovereign of the self, I need freedom from my own negativity.

Make a list: Of your self-sabotaging beliefs and change them into self-sovereignty mottos.

Personality

In very, very simple terms personality is something on the outside.
What we easily see in others.
A chatty person, a quiet person, a good dancer, a great cook etc.
When we say things like, 'She is chatty', 'He is serious', 'He has got rhythm'… we are usually referring to their personality.

Character

Character is something that is much deeper. We see it only in specific circumstances.
Character is about someone's kindness, honesty, humility, generosity, courage…
Both Personality and Character can be either positive or negative.

Don't be impressed by someone's personality alone, look beyond. Inner character is like a rough diamond that can be polished with charming personality traits.

A man of personality can formulate ideals, but only a man of character can achieve them.
Herbert Read

Exercise: Make a list of your character strengths and the qualities of your personality.

Bigotry

When someone is intolerant or makes fun of people who are different from them, it is bigotry.
Bigotry is based on prejudice, racism, intolerance, chauvinism...
Being a bigot means you believe you are better than someone else.
Bigotry is negative and harmful.

Banter

Sometimes it is nice to be playful and joke with our friends about our differences.
It is part of being light-hearted and not taking things too seriously.
Banter is about using wit and being accepting about the differences.
The purpose of banter is just playfulness.
Banter should be positive, light and harmless.

Know the difference between Bigotry and Banter.
When you engage in banter know what the limits are, so it does not become disparaging to someone else.

Banter is playfulness whereas bigotry is disparaging.

Try this: Be playful with your friends about your differences but be light-hearted and maintain respect and regard at all times.

Self-conceited

Self-conceited people are not comfortable with who they are. They want to appear better, more powerful, and more intelligent than they actually are. They have great difficulty in acknowledging their weaknesses. They try to hide their shortcomings by acting overconfident. They behave in an arrogant manner.
They pretend that they are better than others.

Self-confident

Self-confident people are comfortable with who they are. They know their strengths and their weaknesses. They do not hide their flaws.
Self-confident people do not think they are better than others and do not try to project a superior image. They feel a sense of comfort with who they are and have no desire to be better than others.

It is a fine line between confidence, overconfidence and conceitedness.
It is good to be a confident person. It is not so good to become conceited.

The difference between conceit and confidence is that Conceit is just bragging about blowing your own trumpet. Confidence means you can not only play your instrument very well but you also know that you have the skill.

Think about: Your behaviour – when are you confident and when are you acting out of arrogance?

Diagnosis

In the medical world
identifying the exact ailment or disease is the diagnosis.
In everyday life sometimes we get too hung up on the problem or the issue. We keep going round and round in circles dissecting and diagnosing... just because we like to label things and pigeonhole everything.
In life diagnosis is not enough; finding a label for something is only half the matter.
When you are not well, just knowing what you have is not enough. You then have to take the right medication in order to get better.

Prognosis

In the medical world
understanding how the particular illness will be in the future is its prognosis.
It is about knowing what the ailment will do to you in the future so that the right type of treatment can be recommended.
In everyday life it is good to have a future view of the problems that are left without solving. The relationships that are neglected, the little talks that are avoided... the small issues that have the potential to become big...

In the medical world both diagnosis and prognosis are equally important.
Accurate diagnosis and prognosis help to devise the best treatment plan for a patient.
In everyday life, once we have identified the problem it is better to understand how to deal with it and move forward, rather than spending too much time on trying to label who is to be blamed.

In life diagnosis is not always possible; there are things we cannot put labels on.
However, we pretty much know the prognosis for most things – things never remain the same, everything changes.

Suggestion: When you next have a problem with someone, try not to focus too much on who is to be blamed or whose fault it was... Try first to see ahead into the future... If the problem remains, what would happen in the future with you and that person? Once you are able to see the future perspective... you will be surprised how diminished the problem will actually become.

Health

Health is generally referred to as physical fitness. Health means absence of infirmity or disease.
Everyone is very conscious of their physical fitness these days.
Almost everyone knows about the benefits of regular exercise, fruit and veg diet, blood pressure, cholesterol awareness, alcohol units, stopping smoking...

Well-being

Well-being is more than just physical health. Well-being is not merely the absence of disease but it is overall wellness of the human being. It is about living a healthy life with a good balance of physical, mental, emotional, social and spiritual dimensions.

Some people are physically fit, yet they deeply dislike their own body and are constantly trying to change its shape or form. They might have physical health, but are they well?

Good physical health is not the only component needed for a 'healthy life'.
A healthy life is the overall physical, mental, emotional, social and spiritual well-being.

Exercise: Create a monthly timetable for all dimensions – physical, mental, emotional, social and spiritual well-being. Put in activities for each section. Regularly do exercise/activities to maintain good health in each dimension.

Explicit

Some people are explicit in their communication. They don't care much about the person in front. They deliberately use rude, vulgar, insulting and offensive language. They feel because everyone has a right to express themselves however they like, they can be offensive and rude. They think that explicit behaviour or language displays their confidence.

Deliberately offending and insulting people has nothing to do with self-confidence. Rude and explicit language is more about attention-seeking than self-expression.

Expressive

Self-expression is expression of your personality, your feelings, opinions, what you like, what matters to you...

One can express themselves in numerous ways. Through dressing style, through work, through art, through music, through writing and also through speech.

Expression is about communicating not about offending, insulting, shocking, or seeking attention.

It's a fine line between being expressive and being explicit but isn't it perhaps better to express yourself in a way that does not offend others.

Frank and explicit – that is the right line to take when you wish to conceal your own mind and confuse the minds of others.
Benjamin Disraeli

Think about: In which ways do you express yourself? Think about your dressing style/choice of music/books you read... how can you express yourself more?

Snobbish

Sometimes people think that being snobbish, unapproachable and standoffish exhibits some kind of importance or class. Being stuck-up, arrogant, unsympathetic or snooty is neither posh nor upper class.

Stiff Upper Lip

'Stiff upper lip' is to do with being a self-composed and a sober person.
It is classy behaviour to be keep one's cool in difficult circumstances and not be consumed by wild outbursts of anger, fury, hatred or loathing towards others.
It does not mean being cold-hearted or uncaring; it just means to be in control of one's emotions and emotional state where it is appropriate.

Snobbish and stiff upper lip are two different things.
One is about being stuck-up and the other is about being self-composed.
Which one is classier?

The notion of stiff upper lip has perhaps been misunderstood throughout time.
Maintaining one's inner equanimity is not snobbish.

Think about: A time when you may have acted 'snobbish'. What was the real reason behind your behaviour? Also think about a time you were able to maintain your cool despite the aggravating situation.

Emotion

Emotions can happen as a reaction to events, or at times for no apparent reason. We can get angry, anxious, excited, frightened, sad, nervous, furious, etc.
Emotions are powerful and have a huge effect on us. Sometimes negative emotions are so powerful that they can completely drain us.
Emotions can sometimes be overwhelming as we feel consumed by them and don't quite know how to deal with them.

E-motion

E-motion is 'energy' in motion. Whenever you feel highly emotional about something just remember that emotions are just 'energy' in motion and so they will pass... It is not good to be consumed by emotions. Strong emotions drain our positive energy. It is also not good to suppress them, but to let them flow knowing that it's just energy that is passing and it is not solid or permanent.

It is good to take some time to understand what triggers your emotions.
It's also good to know emotions pass and they are not permanent states of being.

Emotions don't last.
It is a good idea not to base anything permanent on something that is temporary.
Don't make irreversible decisions when you are angry, sad, upset or excited.

Suggestion: Next time you are feeling emotional about something, sit down and just write about all your feelings and everything related to the matter. Expressive writing can help in releasing and calming the emotions.

Life Expectancy

Live expectancy is a measure of how long we are expected to live.
Different countries have different life expectancy.
For example, it is said that Japan has one of the highest life expectancies. The average age of how long people live there is about 86 years.
Nigeria on the other hand is said to have a lower life expectancy. The average age of how long people live there is about 54 years.
Life Expectancy is about the length of our lives.

Life Satisfaction

Life satisfaction is a measure of how satisfied we are with our lives.
There are also many surveys and research findings that show that different countries seem to have different levels of life satisfaction.
Switzerland and Denmark come up as amongst the most satisfied countries, and Syria and Afghanistan come up amongst the least satisfied countries.
Life Satisfaction is about the quality of our lives.

Somehow average life expectancy seems to be increasing.
We are living longer but are we living happier?

We have added years to life, but not life to years.
George Carlin

Suggestion: Write your own fantasy obituary. Write down all the things you wish you had done with your life. Write down how you would like to be remembered. Write down all the qualities you would like people to remember you for. Put it away and reread it after a week.

Self-conscious

Self-conscious is a term used to usually describe someone who is perhaps insecure, shy, timid, uncomfortable, tense, tongue-tied, withdrawn...
Someone who is also constantly worried about what others think of them.
Self-consciousness can come from not knowing oneself. Not being sure of who you are and what you want.

Self-aware

Self-aware people are confident and have a good clear understanding of their self...
They have a good overview of what they want, what their personal needs are and what things they need to develop about themselves.
They value other people's opinions but they don't get negatively affected by them.

We can all be self-conscious from time to time; however, to be consumed constantly by thoughts of how others see us or what they think about us is a waste of time.
It is more important to observe what you think of yourself before you start to worry about what others think of you.
Self-awareness is the first step towards any positive change and development.

What is necessary to change a person is to change his awareness of himself.
Abraham Maslow

Exercise: List five things that are guaranteed to make you laugh. List five that make you self-conscious.

Pain	**Suffering**
Pain is physiological; it's a physical experience. In illness we feel physical pain. Physical pain is nature's way of alerting us that something is wrong somewhere in the body. Some level of pain is inevitable; it is part of our physical existence.	Suffering is our psychological response to pain. It is our interpretation of the situation. Suffering can exist even in the absence of pain and it can also be completely absent despite tremendous pain. Suffering is a choice.

Pain is part of our human existence, suffering is part of our spiritual journey.
Accept pain, so that suffering can diminish.

Pain is inevitable, suffering is optional.
Zen proverb

Suggestion: Think about someone who is in pain or is suffering. Do a 10-minute kindness meditation and send them love and healing vibration.

Numb

Feeling emotionally numb is a sign of depression.
This can happen after a traumatic experience; the person just shuts down and becomes completely 'dissociated' with everything and everyone around them.
They do not feel anything and do not engage with anything.
They cannot accept what has happened and in order to avoid the pain they numb themselves towards everything.

Neutralize

To neutralize a traumatic situation is different from becoming 'numb' towards it.
It is not about hiding away from reality or ignoring it, but about accepting it.
However, this is much easier said than done; it can be very difficult to accept the aftermath of trauma.
One way to move into acceptance is to say to yourself, 'This has happened. It just is.'
'It just is' is about accepting what has happened. *'It just is'* is about letting it be, whatever it is, and not focusing on the negative side nor forcing yourself to change it into something positive there and then.
'It just is' allows an interval for feelings to settle and neutralize.

When something traumatic happens, it is quite difficult to immediately focus on the 'positive'.
It is easier at first to neutralize it and see it as something neither good nor bad.
It just is.

It is much easier to move into a positive frame of mind from a neutral place than from a totally negative one.

Think about: Something (nothing major, perhaps a small incident) you are feeling a bit upset about. Think about it and repeat 'It just is' several times. Observe how that feels.

Delusion

Delusion is believing in something that does not exist. It is a pure fantasy. It is belief in something false.
Our beliefs often contribute to our actions, so it is important to check our beliefs.
Believing you are better and superior to everyone else is a delusion.
Such delusions can be harmful.

Confusion

Confusion can be stressful, but at least you know you are confused.
We all get things muddled up at times and we can all be confused about certain situations... at certain times.
Confusion is OK; it is just paving the way for clarity that lies ahead.

It's better to be unsure at times than to be certain of the wrong things.

Confusion relates to the perspective and delusion relates to a belief.
Confusion can sometimes make us see things from a new perspective.
Delusion just makes us stuck in a wrong belief.

Exercise: Next time you are confused about something, take a paper and a pencil and draw a mind map of everything related to it... leave it for some time. Then come back to it and look at it again with fresh eyes... confusion will change into clarity – bingo!

Cure

Cure is about finding a remedy when something has already deteriorated or failed.
When someone already has ill health, it's about restoring it by finding the right treatment and right medication.
Cure is about remedy and restoration.

Prevention

Prevention is about stopping something unpleasant or bad from happening in the first place. In physical health it means preventing occurrence of disease.
It is about doing things in such a way that things don't deteriorate or get worse.
It is about being mindful and conscientious of your actions in the present moment.

We cannot predict everything and some unpleasant things will happen regardless of caution.
However, there are things in life that can be prevented.
Prevention is better than cure.

Prevention is simple.
In physical health it means to eat moderately, drink responsibly, and exercise vigorously.
In mental health it means to share generously, listen patiently, help willingly, laugh heartily and love deeply.
Anonymous

Idea: Write your prevention list related to health. What kind of diet, exercise and activities do you need to engage in now?

IQ

IQ (Intelligence Quotient) is the ability to understand and apply logical reasoning in relation to words, maths, space and abstract concepts.

EQ

EQ (Emotional Quotient) or Emotional Intelligence is the ability to evaluate, understand, perceive and express emotions in a way as to make best use of them.

Emotional Intelligence is simply the common sense that is essential to live in a social world.
We need to focus more on our emotional intelligence, and the good news is that it can be learned and developed.

IQ means you know what went wrong in situations with other people.
EQ means you realize that what went wrong in situations with other people also has a lot to do with you!

Suggestion: Discuss a controversial topic with your friends. Something that is of importance to you and them. For this discussion don't use your logical reasoning, use your EQ instead. The aim of this exercise is to create a stronger bond with your friends and not to prove your intelligence or to prove yourself right. See how you can achieve that.

Swallowing

Everyone is so busy. We hardly have any time to eat. We get so tied up in daily activity that we just swallow food.
We eat fast and we eat quickly. We don't like to waste time. Eating is at times just a daily chore that we have to do.
Even when we are eating something we love, we eat it too quickly; it's just an act of consumption or entertainment.

Savouring

Savouring is about really appreciating what we are eating or drinking.
It is about fully experiencing and tasting every sensation associated with it. The texture, the smell, the taste, the temperature, the feeling...
It is not just about consumption. It is about fully appreciating the food we are eating and being grateful for it.

When we fully savour what we eat, we actually eat less as we feel so satisfied and enriched with the sensations that we need to consume less...
Food gives us life and energy. Food needs to be savoured.
Food is a blessing; appreciate it fully.

Food is a blessing. Treat it like one. Savour it, appreciate it and be grateful for it.
Eat with mindfulness.

Try this: Make yourself a cup of hot chocolate on cold day or a get yourself a glass of cold fresh juice on a hot day. Sit on your sofa comfortably and take tiny sips. Feel the taste and smell the aroma of the drink. Sip slowly. Feel the warmth or the coolness of the drink. Don't gulp it. Drink it very slowly fully enjoying each and every sip you take and feeling gratitude for its blessing.

Variety

There is so much on offer everywhere. So many assortments of everything.
Just in the breakfast section of the supermarket there is a huge selection of different ranges of cereals, muesli, porridge, oats, Pop-Tarts, granola...
Each range has so many brands, each brand has so many flavours...
The variety is enormous.

Choice

Choose one from the following variety –
Coca-Cola, 7up, water, Diet Coke, Fanta, Pepsi, Sprite, Tango...
You may think the variety offers you eight choices.
In reality you have only two choices.
A fizzy drink or water.

Choice is different from variety.
Don't be fooled by the enormous variety on offer.
Learn to discern the real choices.

Life is about making choices.
Do your best to make good choices even with what appears to be little things.
Fizzy drink or Water?

Think about: One choice you have made recently. What made you choose that instead of the other?

Disease

Disease is sickness of the body. It is physical illness that needs treatment.
Diseases can be caused by viruses or bacteria or infection or bugs etc.
Having a disease means you are physically ill. Your body is not OK physically.
A body that has a disease needs medication.

Dis-ease

When there is nothing wrong with the actual physical health of the body but you don't like your body and are not 'at ease' with it, you have dis-ease.
There is a lot of dis-ease around. People are constantly looking for physical modification of the body in order to feel 'at ease' with themselves. Compulsive shopping for clothes and plastic surgery are all on the rise.
When one has 'dis-ease', the body does not need medication or operations; it just needs to be appreciated for what it is.

Body conscious mentality is perpetually at dis-ease with the appearance of the body.
It is obsessed with the way it looks and fails to appreciate the awesome beauty with which it actually functions.

Whenever there is dis-ease with the body for the way it looks,
It does not need medication to fix it.
It just needs appreciation.
Love your body, don't be at dis-ease with it.

Think about: Which are your favourite parts that you love about your body?

Doubt

Doubt is when you keep digging up the seed every day to check why it is not growing. It is not going to grow if it is dug up every day… is it? Doubt stops things from growing.

Dedication

Dedication is when you leave the seed planted in the ground. You water it regularly and nurture it. You remain patient and give it time to grow. Dedication is about perseverance and patience.

If we want to achieve something we have to be dedicated towards it.

If we keep doubting it, it will never happen.

Doubt has killed more dreams than failure ever will.
Unknown

Exercise: Think of an idea you have had for some time. Write a paragraph about what's really stopping you. Write another paragraph about what's possible and how far could you go with it.

Give Up

We all have habits that we think we must stop.
I must give up smoking, it is damaging my health.
I must give up watching junk TV, it wastes my time.
I must give up office gossip, it is affecting my professionalism.
So on...

Gain It

Let's start thinking of what we gain when we start taking up new activities and habits.
I will gain better health by running three times weekly.
I will gain time for painting on Monday evening as I won't be watching trash TV.
I will get better at my job as I will not be engaging in useless gossip.

It is better to think about gaining something nice than telling yourself to give up something.

Stop thinking about what you must give up.
Start thinking about what you are gaining.

Try this: Think of one habit/activity that you want to give up; think of another thing you can replace it with. Then construct a 'gain it' statement. Repeat that to yourself several times. Visualize yourself actually doing it. How does it feel?

Comparison

Comparison is about comparing ourselves with others ambiguously.
He is better than me.
She is happier than me.
They live a better life than us.
Such thinking is useless and often not even true. It serves no purpose in our life. It is not good to compare yourself to others.
Everyone has a different life and what seems better or worse is about their life, not yours.

Precision

Precision is better than comparison.
He is better than me.
Better at what specifically?
She is happier than me.
Happier in which way exactly?
They live a better life than us.
What elements are better about their life?
Often precision questions will make us realize what seems better for others is usually better for them, not us.

Grass seems greener on the other side.
In fact grass is greener where it is watered.
Stop comparing your life with others.
Change general comparisons to precision questions.
Ask self-precision questions to discover what exactly others do or have that you like.
Often you can do something about it yourself.

A flower does not think of comparing itself with the flower next to it.
It just blooms.
Unknown

Think of: One person you compare yourself with, then ask yourself some precision questions.

Blender

A blender mixes liquid and solid stuff together.
When you are creating something new, writing a story, imagining the script of a movie you need to be highly innovative.
You need to mix facts and fiction together to come up with something new.
Use your mental blender, create a new blend and be creative.

Sieve

A sieve separates liquid and solid stuff.
When you are dealing with relationship problems with someone, a colleague, a friend, family, children... you need to have your facts right.
You need to separate facts from fiction. What actually happened and what were just assumptions, misjudgements, and misinterpretations...
Use your mental sieve to separate facts from fiction.

Learning is not just about focusing on facts, it is also about knowing how to mix fact and fiction to create something new and innovative.
Different forms of literature, media and politics are just variations of blends of the two.

The line between fact and fiction is a thin one, but we need both in our lives. We need to know when and how to mix them up to create something new, and also when and how to separate them to illuminate what is true.

Suggestion: Write a short story. Blend some facts with fiction. Use what you know to create something new.

Tale of Woe

What's your story?
A tragedy where you play the role of a victim in which you suffer and endure pain and grief all throughout your life...
A melodrama filled with heartbreak of losing lovers or filled with anguish of unfulfilled dreams?
How does your story end?

Tale of Wow!

Is your story a comedy, a romance or action novel... filled with Wow moments?
What roles do you play – a lover, a teacher, a warrior, an entertainer...?
There is loads of joy and vigour in the story. There is also pain and difficulties but you play your role with determination, grit and with love.
How would you want it to end?
It is your story, you can write it anyway you like.

No one else can tell your story as well as you can yourself.

We read so many stories and watch so many films.
Sometimes we forget that our own story is the greatest story of all.
Cherish your story.

Idea: Write a short one-page story of your life. Choose how you want to write it. A comedy, action, mystery, suspense, romance... What are the Wow moments in it?

Absorbing Germs

When someone says things to you that you don't like, do you automatically get offended or upset?
Would you willingly take viruses, germs or bugs from someone and fall ill?
Receiving someone's bad comments and insults is like willingly taking bugs and germs into your system.
When people say negative things just remember that you don't need to absorb everything.

Receiving Flowers

When someone says good things and gives compliments, accept them like beautiful flowers. Let their aroma add perfume to your life, just like fresh flowers add fragrance to your room.
Decorate them in your mind and water them, let them last a while.
Don't forget to say thank you to the person who gave them.

Insults and invalid criticism are like germs, and compliments are like flowers.
Germs make people sick, flowers make people happier.
Don't willingly take germs from others, receive flowers instead.
Choice is yours.

When people give you compliments decorate them in your mind. Let them be like flowers that add fragrance to your room for a long time.

Suggestion: Notice when people give compliments to you – do you just brush them off or do you accept them and really let them add fragrance to your life?

Rubbish Bin

Do you treat your body like a rubbish bin? Do you put dead animals, stale, processed, unnatural, artificial stuff in it? Do you overeat just because you don't want to throw leftover food in the bin, so instead you end up treating your body like one?

Temple

Do you treat your body like a temple? A temple is a sacred and pure place. You would only take fresh, natural, nutritious, wholesome food into the temple.

Your body is not a dumping ground but a sacred sanctuary and food is not just consumption; it is nourishment for your physical being.

Think of your stomach as a sacred space.
You would not want to put unnatural, artificial, processed, stale stuff in it.
You would only ever want to put pure and natural things in it.

They say you are what you eat so don't be fast, cheap, easy or fake.
Unknown

Exercise: Organize your kitchen cupboards and fridge. Get rid of all the artificial and processed food items. Make sure you have fresh, healthy and natural food items in your kitchen.

Relationships

Independence

Independence means being capable of existing by yourself and being self-reliant.
In individualistic societies independence, especially financial independence is regarded highly. It means being capable of doing things for yourself and not needing other people.
It is good to be self-sufficient, so that we can look after ourselves. However, being too independent can sometimes make us dependent on our own independence. This sometimes means that we actually become scared of needing support from others.

Interdependence

Interdependence is different from independence. It means having the ability to look after ourselves but also being able to collaborate with others.
What does this mean?
This means that we don't just become self-sufficient, we also become self-aware of our limitations.
We are able to value what others can do for us and we have the capability to ask for support.
Interdependence means knowing that at times two heads are better than one.

Too much independence can lead to seclusion and isolation. Everyone needs support at times.

Life doesn't make any sense without interdependence. We need each other, and the sooner we learn that, the better for us all.
Erik Erikson

Try this: Next time you have to fix something in the house or do some decoration ask a friend to help. Do it together and after the completion of the task go out for a meal together.

Stubborn

Stubborn means to stand your ground. It further means to stand your ground 'no matter what'. More often than not a stubborn person knows that they are wrong but they refuse to admit it. To them being right is more important than to have the right solution. Stubbornness is unwillingness to change your mind or your opinion, no matter what.

A stubborn person has no ability to listen to others.

Strong

A strong person also stands their ground. They have the resolve and conviction to stand up for what they believe in. They are tough but at the same time they also remain open-minded. They are humble enough to admit when they are wrong and insightful enough to change their mind for a better solution.

The strength of a strong person comes from the ability to listen to others.

Watch your strong-mindedness; does it sometimes turn into stubbornness?

If you see yourself wanting to appear to be right when you know you are wrong, then you need to examine your stubbornness.

The weakness of a stubborn person comes from inability to change.

The strength of the strong person lies in open-mindedness towards change.

Think about: A time when you were 'standing your ground' about something. Were you being stubborn or were you being strong?

Attachment

Attachment is sometimes confused with love.
Attachment is more about your own neediness than about the other person.
Attachment means identifying with the other person in the form of clinging.
This clinging produces fear that if the person goes away there will be loss of one's own identity. This fear of loss of identity brings anxiety. This anxiety seeks a guarantee that this won't happen. This then becomes a dependency on the person. This is about one's own neediness.
Attachment is conditional as it changes when the needs change.
It takes more than it gives.

Love

Love is the utmost finest pursuit of mankind. It has many forms and expressions...
In contrast to attachment, love does not control nor does it cling. It liberates and allows growth. It is something that is lasting and is not dependent on circumstances nor is conditional. Even when someone goes away or they move on... the deep positive feeling and unconditional positive regard for them remains.
Love does not seek guarantees as it is not about taking; it is more about giving.

Ask yourself, are you looking for love? Or are you actually looking for someone to love you?
Love cannot be taken or demanded; it can only be experienced by being love itself.

Attachment concerns itself with taking.
Love's only concern is acceptance.
Attachment wants happiness.
Love gives happiness.

Do: Write down your own definition of love (about 150 words).

Issue

We often say or hear things like, 'I have this or that issue at work and I am feeling very stressed about it.'
An issue usually refers to a problem or concern. Problems or concerns usually cause worry and stress.
Nobody likes stress or worry.

Event

An event is an occurrence or an activity.
There are many events taking place simultaneously all around us.
We don't attend every event under the sun.
We choose which events we want to attend.
An event is just an occurrence.
It is not something to worry about; it is not a problem.

When something occurs in your life, just pause and ask yourself, 'Is this an event or an issue?'
Don't make every little thing that happens into a problem or something to worry about.

Not every event that takes place in your life is an issue. Don't turn it into one.

Think about: Past few recent occurrences that were just events but you turned them into an issue or problem. How would you see them differently now?

Worry

We often hear statements such as, 'I am so worried about him/her that I can't even eat or sleep well these days.'
By this statement we interpret that this person cares a lot about the other person.
We have to wonder why 'not eating or sleeping' translates as care for the other person.
Would the other person not want you to eat or sleep well?
How would 'not eating or sleeping' help the other person?
What is the point of such worry?

Care

When we care about someone or something it means we are interested in them and what is happening to them.
We want to know if the person is OK and if we could help in some way.
Caring means being thoughtful, attentive and considerate towards the other person or the situation.
Care does not mean becoming restless, anxious, upset yourself in relation to the concern for the other person. You might just be adding to their distress rather than helping them...

Worry does not mean care.
Worry is useless. It does not help the situation or the person.
When you show worry, you are actually just showing your own fear.

Worry less. Care more.

Think about: Who are you worried about at the moment? In which ways could you worry less and care more for them?

Hearing

Hearing is simply the act of perceiving sound by the ear. Hearing is a physiological process; it is passive.
Hearing just happens. It is an involuntary process to do with how sound waves influence the fluid in the ears and send messages to the brain.
Hearing is a physical ability.

Listening

Listening is a psychological process. It's to do with how well we understand what is being said. Listening is voluntary and we choose to listen.
Listening is about being patient, not interrupting, and remaining fully attentive, being interested... and not judging.
Good listening has to be learned; it's an acquired skill.

Most of the time when we listen we hear a few words and we jump into the editing room of our mind to prepare an answer or action before we have paid attention to everything that is being said...
Most of us have been gifted with the ability to hear, but do we listen correctly?
We may hear perfectly well but are we sometimes 'hard of listening'...

Listening with the intention to reply is just about you. Better to listen with the desire to really understand the other person.

Idea: Create a listening hour ritual with your partner (or a close friend). For one hour don't speak; just listen, then swap.

Transactional Love

The love we all talk about in our daily life is perhaps 'transactional love'.
In reality when we say 'I love you' to someone we actually mean:
I love you, only if you love me back.
I love you, only when you do X or buy X for me.
I love you, only if you behave the way I like.
This type of love is given and received as a transaction; in order to give we need to get something first.

Unconditional Love

Unconditional love means to love someone without conditions.
It means:
I love you anyway, even when sometimes you don't love me back.
I love you anyway, even if sometimes I don't like when you do X.
I love you anyway, even when you don't do X for me.
Unconditional love is acceptance but it doesn't mean it approves of everything.
It just means it has the capability to see beyond the behaviour of the person and love the person unconditionally regardless of what they do or don't do.

We all want unconditional love.
Some of us dream that one day someone will come along and love us 'just the way we are'.
Let's ask ourselves first, how conditional is our own love?
What do we want from the other person and how would we want them to behave?

The greatest thing you can do is to give the gift of unconditional love and acceptance to someone else.

Think about: Two people you love. What conditions, if any, do you attach to your love for them?

Sympathy

Sympathy means we recognize someone's emotional distress and we feel the need to acknowledge it by giving advice, expressing concern and condolences appropriate to their plight or misfortune. Sympathy is about our own need to express concern.

Empathy

Empathy is understanding the situation someone is in, plus the ability to feel what they are feeling. It is a connection with the feelings of the person in that particular situation.
It is a deep understanding of what someone is going through and the ability to let them know that you understand them without the need to give advice or express pity.

When we are with someone who is not in a good situation, it is good to be aware of what we are offering. Our sympathy or empathy?

Empathy is walking a mile in someone's shoes; sympathy is feeling sorry their feet hurt.
Unknown

Suggestion: Visit someone who is not well or is going through a rough patch. Just be with them, empathize with them.

Provoking

When you are talking to different people they all seem to get irritated.
You say something and they get angry or upset.
If this happens a lot, then it is to do with your manner not them.
You need to be aware of the intention of your communication.
Are you trying to stimulate their thinking or trying to provoke a reaction from them?

Evoking

It is good to say something that makes the other person remember something nice.
Remembering something nice evokes pleasant feelings.
When you are talking to people it is good to try to evoke nice feelings rather than get them irritated or upset.
When you are with your friends, from time to time it is nice to recall some nice memories from the past to evoke some pleasant feelings.

The truth is nobody likes being provoked.
Everyone would rather be evoked by pleasant memories.

Does your conversation have the power to evoke something pleasant in others?
Or does it merely provoke them?
It is better to stir up positive vibes than to get someone upset and angry!

Exercise: Next time you are with a friend or a family member, recall a pleasant shared memory and talk about it like you are revisiting the past. Enjoy talking about it together.

Expecting

Expectations are about our own need. It is our need for people to behave in a particular way or to do things in the way we want.

We all have expectations from other people but we have to remember that generally everyone has their own way of doing things and our way is not the only way.

Quite often in relationships when expectations are not met it leads to resentment, hurt and disappointment.

Expecting things to turn out a specific way can lead to disappointment as often things evolve in their own way.

Accepting

In relationships accepting someone the way they are is often the key to bliss.

This is easier said than done.

We all have our own ways of doing things, and more often than not we get disappointed when someone does not do or behave the way we wanted them to.

Acceptance means being OK with how someone is; this does not mean being passive or tolerant of bad behaviour.

It means allowing people to be who they are regardless of your own preferences.

Acceptance is rooted in the present moment, to receive and accept whatever is happening now and to create the best possible response to it.

Expecting means wanting others to be exactly like you and for everything to happen as you imagine.

Accepting means knowing people are all different and that life cannot be predicted.

Acceptance -> Happiness

Expectation -> Unhappiness

Suggestion: Spend some time with a person you normally don't get along with. Focus on accepting them the way they are.

Relationships

Most romantic relationships start out on a high and everything looks perfect. As time progresses some things change within the relationship and it doesn't quite feel the same as it did in the beginning and some ambiguity creeps in...
It feels different yet familiar.
It is the same person we fell in love with but the feelings are different.
The nature of the feelings change, electricity and sparks somewhat diminish... yet there is a newfound familiarity with the person.
Some people think that this means there is something not right with the relationship or that it is fading or diminishing.

Relation-shifts

We all want when we find the perfect relationship that it will remain exactly the same forever. This cannot happen. Things change.
We think when the nature of the relationship starts to change something is wrong with it.
We get worried and start to question the relationship.
Worry brings doubt and doubt starts to affect the relationship in a negative way. Things then start going downhill.
Change is inevitable; rather than seeing change in a relationship as a negative thing, it is best to accept it as a natural thing.
It is just a shift, a relation-shift.

All relationships keep changing. Romantic relationship changes from passion to a quieter, deeper love.
Relationship with children changes from care giving to care receiving at later stages in life.
This is not about better or worse... they are just relation-shifts.

All relationships change over time, they have relation-shifts. Do not be afraid of the change. See it as a progressive shift.

Think about: Your relationship with your parents. How has it changed over the years? What is different now?

Neediness

Neediness is when you are not OK with yourself and need the other person in the relationship to 'make you OK'. Neediness comes from not knowing what you want and what you are lacking. It is expecting that the other person should know exactly what you need and make everything OK for you.
If you are not OK with yourself, how can someone on the outside go inside your head and make things OK there?
You have to sort it out yourself.

Need

In a relationship, we all have some fundamental needs. The need to be treated with respect, the need to express ourselves, the need to give and receive love etc.
It is OK to want these basic needs met in a relationship as long as your sense of self-worth does not come before the relationship itself.

Everyone has human needs, we want to share companionship, connection, hugs, touch, laughter... we are social beings and these needs are natural.
Neediness on the other hand is not about sharing, it is about wanting from the other person.

In a relationship needs can be met; however, neediness persists.

Exercise: List all the things you think you want in a relationship. Identify which ones are basic needs and which ones are perhaps about neediness.

Obligation

We all have responsibilities towards other people. These can be towards our children, elderly parents, colleagues, spouse, friend etc.

Often when we do things for them we see it as our obligation. We feel liable as per our duty. We feel a sense of compulsion because we know we 'have' to do those things for them. When we do things with a sense of compulsion it almost becomes a burden. The pleasure of doing things for others goes away. It then becomes just a chore.

Gift

A gift is a present we give to people on special occasions. We enjoy giving gifts and people enjoy receiving gifts. Gifts are fun.

When we are in the process of choosing a gift, we think about the person and picture what they would like.

Similarly when doing something for someone, if we add that extra bit of care and consideration as if it were a special occasion and as if what we are doing for them is not a duty or chore but a gift, then it becomes more than just obligation. It becomes joy.

There is a difference when we ***have*** to do something for someone as compared to when we ***want*** to do something for someone.

When you need to do something for someone, rather than thinking about it as an obligation or duty, think about it as a gift.

Exercise: Next time you need to do something for someone consider that you are giving them a gift. Give it with joy and see how different it will feel to them as well as yourself.

Gullible

Is 'giving till it hurts' a good thing? If giving is causing you pain then surely it cannot be right. What good is giving if you yourself are not going to be OK? If you are not going to be OK, how could you possibly be in the position to give to others? Being gullible is when someone is taking advantage of you unduly and you feel hurt. Giving should not hurt.

Generous

Generosity is good. The joy lies in giving not in receiving. We should give, it is good to give. People think to be generous is only about giving stuff – presents or money and only the rich can afford to be generous. Giving is not only about giving material things, it is about giving who you are.
Give your qualities and your virtues. Give kindness, compassion, love… empathy. Be generous; being generous does not hurt or cause pain.

If your giving hurts you, you need to observe whether what you are doing is an act of generosity or to do with your inability to say no…

We make a living by what we get, but we make a life by what we give.
Winston Churchill

Try this: Give one quality consciously per day. Example: Kindness, Appreciation, Enthusiasm, Humour, Creativity…

Closed Questions

We all know about the typical 'closed questions'. The questions that result in a yes or no answer.

Here, what is meant by a closed question is a question that we ask someone when we aren't interested in hearing the answer.

An everyday closed question is: 'How are you?'

Do we really care how someone is? Or are we asking for the sake of being polite?

When a question is asked for the sake of asking but there is no interest in the answer, it is a closed question. It closes real communication.

Open Questions

Generally these are questions that cannot be answered by one word answers, or a yes or a no. They require more than a word to answer them.

Here, what is meant by an open question is a question you ask and then allow yourself to be really open to the nature of the answer.

So even if you hear an answer that you don't like or were not expecting, you remain open to the different point of view.

Sometimes we ask questions and we only want to hear the answer that we want. We are not open to a different point of view.

A real open question is when we remain truly open to the answer.

The art of real conversation is to know the true nature of your questions.

It's not the answers we get in life but the questions we ask that matter.

Practice: Keeping a specific person in mind, write down three real open questions, and next time you have the opportunity, ask them.

Aggressive

Aggressiveness in conversations is about interrupting and taking over someone's conversation. It is also about not showing any concern for others and their need to express themselves in the conversation. It is about trying to prove others wrong and yourself right so much so that you start making disparaging comments about them.

Assertive

Assertiveness is about observing yourself.
In conversations it is about making yourself heard without the need to prove others wrong. It is about maintaining respect for others, whilst you put across your viewpoint with confidence.

In a conversation, if you keep asserting yourself to the point that you stop caring about the viewpoint or feelings of others, you have crossed the line into aggression.

Assertive behaviour respects both parties equally.
Aggressive behaviour does not care about the well-being of others.

Practice: Identify a topic that you generally shy away from during a conversation. Start the discussion at the next opportunity. Remain assertive during the conversation but do not become aggressive.

Impressing

When we do something or say something solely to seek admiration from others we are trying to impress them. This need to impress others has become an obsession these days. What we say, what we do, what we wear, what we eat, where we go… everything is done so that others can admire us. This need for doing everything in the light of what others think of us can become so strong that we stop being true to our own authentic self. We see this a lot in social media where some people post photos just to make everyone think highly of them.

Expressing

Expressing is communicating what is important to us. It is important to express ourselves clearly. By expressing ourselves clearly others can understand who we are and what matters to us, and they can see us more accurately. Expressing something is not for the sake of winning approval; it is solely for the sake of sharing our viewpoint and to show who we are as an individual.

Express yourself from the heart, without the neediness to impress anyone.

Work for a cause, not for applause. Live life to express, not to impress.
Don't strive to make your presence noticed, just make your absence felt.
Unknown

Exercise: Discuss a book or a film with your friend. Express your viewpoints of it in a way that they get an understanding of what's important to you. Also find out what is important to them.

Forget

We are told to forget the negativity, the grudges, the regrets, the pain, the hurt, the heartaches... but quite often we also forget the good stuff. Our childhood friends, acts of kindness, loving memories, gentle embraces, stories that granny read, presents we received... all those tiny wonderful things and moments worth remembering, we often forget them.
We often also forget the lessons we had learned through all the negative stuff.

Forgive

We all know the virtues of forgiveness. To forgive is divine. We all know harbouring deep grudges does more harm to us than to the ones who have wronged us. We also know that feeling compassion for others helps us to forgive.
Whilst we may be too busy forgiving others we often omit forgiving our own self.
Feelings of guilt and shame are natural when we feel we haven't lived up to our own potential. However, wallowing in shame without redeeming actions is neither good nor useful.
Time to time we also need to apply self-forgiveness.
Let's not forget to forgive ourselves...

In our quest for forgetting the negative we sometimes end up forgetting the good stuff.
It's good to keep a gratitude diary, to remind us of the good stuff.

Do not forget to be grateful to those who taught you through pain and do remember to forgive yourself for your own mistakes that made you almost insane.

Think about: 1) A loving memory from your childhood. 2) A lesson you learned from something negative. 3) A mistake you made, for which you can now forgive yourself.

Doormat

Doormat is a mat outside the door for people to wipe their shoes on.
Sometimes people have such a deep desire to be liked by everyone that they allow some people to treat them badly.
Are you a people pleaser?
Do you sacrifice your own values whilst trying to please others?
Do you knowingly allow people to behave badly by letting them take advantage of your generosity?
Being a doormat is not about wanting to be helpful to others; it is more about one's own selfish need to be liked.
Doormats like being used as they crave the feeling of being liked and needed by others.
They passively put up with inappropriate behaviour.

Doorman

Doorman stands at the entrance of the building, and opens and closes the door for visitors.
He also provides security and screens who to let in.
Like the doorman be discerning.
Don't let people take advantage of your generosity.
Don't agree to do something for someone if you have to sacrifice your own values.
Don't put up with inappropriate and improper behaviour.
Doorman is polite and courteous to all visitors but at the same time he observes and regulates who should and shouldn't go in.

Doormats cannot stop anybody from coming in.
Doorman has the ability to stop the wrong people from going in.

Nice is good, but letting go of personal values in order to appear nice all the time to everyone turns one into a habitual doormat. Better to be a Doorman than a Doormat.

Think about: Someone who you had allowed in the past to mistreat you. What would you do differently now?

Infatuation

When someone says they have fallen in 'love' with someone at first sight, they are referring to being infatuated by someone.
Infatuation has more to do with our own desired image of someone in our head rather than their actual real self. We often put the object of our infatuation on a pedestal. We unconsciously assign them qualities that they may not in reality have. With time when we discover the real person behind our own rose-tinted glasses, we realize they are not the exact match of what we wanted or imagined them to be. We then stop 'loving' them.
In a way infatuation is a 'mock-up' of real love. We think it is love, but actually infatuation is about the fantasy of love in our own minds.
Infatuation may not last as when the idealized person in the head becomes a 'real' person, the fascination dissipates.

Love

Love blossoms over time.
It deepens with real understanding of the other person and with true awareness of own self.
Love doesn't wear rose-tinted glasses. It has 20/20 vision. It sees everything and embraces the other allowing them to be who and what they are.
The nature of love may change but love does not stop, as it is not held by conditions or circumstances.
Romantic love may change into compassionate love and compassionate love may change into consummate love, but true love remains unconditional.

If you are seeking love then you need to know the difference between infatuation and love.

Infatuation is when you find someone absolutely perfect. Love is when you realize they aren't perfect and it doesn't matter.
Unknown

Idea: Go to a place with your partner (friend/relative) where they really want to go. Express your love verbally, non-verbally, with hugs, kisses, however is appropriate to them and your relationship with them. Let them know your love for them will remain unconditional.

Sacrificing

Sacrificing something for others involves neglecting your own needs. When own needs are neglected any giving that occurs comes from the place of scarcity.

Scarcity assumes that there is not enough, and in order to fulfil the needs of the other, one has to give up something of themselves.

When you give up something for someone, it almost becomes compulsory for the other person to accept it. Once the sacrifice is accepted it then seeks recognition.

Sacrificing may initially mean well by giving, but it ends up actually needing from the other.

Giving

Giving comes from the place of abundance. It is from the place of understanding that there is enough for everyone. It is about sharing what you have with others.

Giving does not expect anything in return.

Giving is an offering to someone, it is not an obligation for them to accept. It is entirely their choice if they want to accept your offering or not. It cannot be forced upon someone and has no ego attached to it.

Giving happens from the place of fulfilment rather than from a place of scarcity.

When one is fulfilled then they can give unconditionally.

You can only ever provide something of value to others by giving who you are, not sacrificing who you are.

Don't sacrifice yourself too much,
because if you sacrifice too much there's nothing else you can give.
Karl Lagerfeld

Suggestion: Do some voluntary work in the community for a charity. Don't sacrifice your time, give your time for supporting their cause.

Coexistence

Some couples live together under the same roof but are mentally in different places. They stay tied to each other just by everyday functionality of life. They share rent, costs, bills, and other living expenses. They just physically exist side by side, but they are not really living together. They just endure and continue their existence with each other without any true connection between them.

Relationship

A relationship is the way two people are connected. The important thing is the quality of that connection. Between a man and a woman or two partners, this is about the way they regard and behave with each other. It is based upon respect and love for each other rather than just sharing costs and functionality of daily life.

A relationship is not about the habitat, it is about the heart.

Living under one roof does not automatically become a relationship between a man and a woman.
That is just coexistence and coexistence is just logistics.
Relationship is beyond logistics, it's about love...

Suggestion: Think about a couple who you think have an amazing relationship. Interview them together, ask them questions about how they create and maintain their wonderful relationship.

Frankness

To be frank is to be open and direct. To be open and direct are considered expressions of transparency and altruism. However, in most cases frankness is actually about the need to offload your own opinion. Frankness doesn't really care how it will affect the other person or whether it will benefit them at all. It is just about you. A person who is being frank knows that it may hurt the listener but he/she doesn't really care as the motive is just saying what he/she needs to say.

Frankness often hurts the other person.

Honesty

Honesty is a gift for the person you care for. That is why you want to give them the gift of your honesty.

Honesty doesn't hurt as it is coming from a place of compassion and benevolence.

When someone is being honest, they care how it will affect the other person, as it is more about the other person and not about the need to offload one's own opinion.

When being honest the words are chosen kindly to 'ensure' a positive effect.

The person, who is being honest, knows it is their responsibility not to hurt the other.

In any communication the most important thing is the 'intention' of the exchange.

Frankness and honesty have completely different intentions.

Frankness doesn't care if it hurts the other person or affects them negatively. Its only concern is voicing self-opinion towards the other.

Frankness doesn't care but honesty is kind and caring.

Tell the truth but do it honestly, don't just be frank about it.

Think about: A time when you were frank with someone. What effect did that have on them? How would you deliver the same message now?

Relationship Busters

There are three main relationship busters:

- Need to change the other person
- Expecting the other person to make us happy
- Taking: wanting praise, validation, devotion...

Relationship Boosters

Three main relationship boosters are:

- Accepting the other person as they are
- Taking the responsibility for our own happiness
- Giving: gratitude, appreciation, compassion, love...

The expectation that the other person will make us happy busts relationships.
Best way to boost any relationship is first taking responsibility for our own happiness.

Most people enter a relationship in order to get something: They're trying to find someone who's going to make them feel good.
In reality, the only way a relationship will last is if you see your relationship as a place that you go to give and not a place that you go to take.
Anthony Robbins

Try this: Keep a handful of relationship boosters with you at all times. A thank you, a smile, a compliment, a joke, a hug... these are all relationship boosters. Pick one and use it every time you need a relationship booster. Which other relationship boosters can you think of?

Debate	**Dialogue**
Debate is when you listen to the other person in order to prove them wrong. Debate is 'against' each other and is about searching for differences. The goal of a debate is winning.	Dialogue happens when you listen to the other person to communicate better with them. Dialogue is about finding the similarities so you can connect and share viewpoints 'with' each other. The goal of a dialogue is a better understanding of each other.

In relationships sometimes we lose sight of what is important.
Is it important to be right or is it more important to be understanding?
When couples argue sometimes they turn it into a debate.
They both want to prove that they are right and the other is wrong.
Debate serves no purpose for them; a good dialogue, however, can resolve things easily.
Debate is just about ego, and the need to win.
Dialogue is actually about the relationship.

Immature people always want to win an argument, even at the cost of a relationship.
Mature people understand that it's sometimes better to lose an argument and win a relationship.
Chinese proverb

Suggestion: Next time you are arguing with your partner about something... use these phrases: I am listening, tell me more...; I see what you are saying...; I never thought of it that way...

Depreciate

When something depreciates it reduces in its value.
There is a reduction or decrease in its former worth.

Appreciate

When something appreciates, it means, it increases in its significance or value.
For example, when capital, currency, stocks, bonds appreciate, what it means is that their price or monetary value has gone up.
To appreciate something is to recognize that something is of value; when something is recognized as valuable its worth goes up.

In relationships -> Nil Appreciation leads to -> Depreciation.
When you appreciate, respect, cherish and acknowledge someone in your life then
the energy between you becomes more positive.
Appreciation = Appreciation

Appreciation is a wonderful thing:
It makes what is excellent in others belong to us as well.
Voltaire

Try this: Don't just say a one-worded 'thanks'; be more detailed and descriptive in your appreciation.
Example: 'I really appreciate your insightful comments on my works. They helped me to clarify my objectives.'

Trial

Trial is a kind of experiment.
Something to try before
deciding upon something or
making up your mind.
Many couples get into a
relationship as a trial, to 'see
how it goes'.
Can anything ever become
successful with only a hesitant
half-hearted effort?
It is not a good idea to treat
relationships like trials.
The future of the relationship
may indeed be uncertain but
it is important to put your
very best effort into it rather
than treat it like a doubtful
involvement.

Commitment

Commitment is the quality of
being dedicated to something
completely.
A relationship or even a job.
In a probationary period
if one thinks 'unless I get
the permanent post there is
no point inputting my best
effort'... then there won't ever
be a permanent post.
Commitment is willingness to
put your best effort, time and
energy towards something
regardless of its longevity. It
is about being present in the
moment and doing your best in
that moment.

Half-hearted involvements and trials do not work in relationships.
Either you are with someone or you are not.

Life is not a trial, you won't be given another chance.
Be committed to it fully, right here, right now.

Think about: Something you agreed to with someone but feel hesitant... when you say 'Yes' to something be totally 100% committed to it. Don't question yourself, don't doubt. Just do it and be committed fully. However, if you feel it's not for you, step out. Don't get involved with something half-heartedly...

Changing Others

Wanting others to change is a lost battle.
The ultimate reality is that people or circumstances don't ever change according to your exact desire...

Changing Self

Changing self is the first step towards true wisdom.
The ultimate power that you have is that you can change something about yourself in order to deal better with the circumstances or people.

Whenever there is some difficulty or a problem in a relationship the very first step should be to think, 'What is it about my own attitude that I can change first.'
Some people say it is not good to change yourself for others, but if you don't have the ability to change yourself why would you expect others to change for you?
Changing yourself is not a weakness but a tremendous strength.

Yesterday I was clever, so I wanted to change the world.
Today I am wise, so I am changing myself.
Rumi

Think about: What have you successfully changed about yourself recently that has made a good impact on your life?

Taking Mode

Taking mode comes from a place of being a beggar. A beggar is bankrupt.
A beggar has nothing and wants others to give him something.
It is about wanting others to make us happy first. Wanting others to please us first. Wanting others to love us first. If you have given nothing to others why would you expect others to give to you first?

Giving Mode

Giving mode means I will give my good wishes and gratitude to others no matter how they are towards me or what they do for me.
Giving means not waiting for others to do something for us first.
Giving mode is like being a banker not a beggar. It comes from a place of power rather than dependency.

Taking mode means I will only be nice to people who are nice to me.
Giving mode means I will be nice to people no matter how they choose to treat me.

How people treat you is their karma; how you treat them is yours.
Wayne Dyer

Suggestion: Try to do a random act of kindness for someone you don't usually get along with or for someone who you don't know that well yet.

Tall, Dark and Harming

When the princess does not know herself what she actually wants in a relationship and what she is capable of being herself, she does not have the ability to select the right pursuer and Prince Charming can turn out to be tall, dark and harming.

Tall, Dark and Handsome

Make a list of your own true qualities and the qualities that you want in your prince. Finding the right person is about knowing yourself first, so that it becomes easier to identify the right match. Princes come in all shapes and forms: Tall, Dark and Handsome to Tall, Dark and Harming.

Tall, Dark and Handsome is not just about good looks, it is about character and virtue.

In order to choose your prince correctly and a good match, you have to first know yourself well.

Think about: Your past relationships... 1) What characteristics of your ex were actually harming you? 2) What could you have done differently yourself then?

Penny Wise **People Foolish**

You may have heard the saying 'Penny wise and pound foolish'. It means making decisions to save a small amount of money but losing larger amounts as a result. It can also mean being too focused on money and less focused on other important things in life.

'Penny wise and people foolish' is keeping money as an objective and focus in your interactions with people. People foolish means being so preoccupied about saving money that you end up damaging relationships because of that.

Sometimes what may appear to be a monetary loss can actually be a gain in a relationship.
Giving financial help to someone in need may mean you might not get your money back, but it could also mean that you have gained a friend forever.

In pursuit of saving pennies, it is important not to lose people. Saving money is not a bad thing, but losing important people in your life because of that is surely not a good thing.
It's OK at times to lose money it is never OK to lose a good friend.

Do: Treat a friend or a family member with something they normally don't do/buy for themselves. Don't focus too much on the amount of expenditure; it should be something you can afford easily. Focus on how much they will enjoy it.

Difficult People

We often associate our problems with 'difficult people'. We find that some people are difficult and we end up thinking that our problems are because of them.

Problems are just situations that have some difficulty and they need to be dealt with, solved or overcome. We all face day-to-day, big and small problems. They are just part of life.

Different People

People are human beings. A human being is an individual with their own set of values and their own way of conducting themselves in this world.

No two people are exactly the same. All people are different.

Problems are difficult, people are just different.
It's good to remember a problem is not the person.
When you have some difficulty with someone, it is better to think of them as someone different from you rather than think of them as the problem.
Don't turn your problems into a person as you can resolve problems, but you cannot change people.

There are no difficult people, just different people.
People are not problems to be solved but they are individuals to be understood.

Think about: A person that you know who is very different from you. What is specifically different that you like about them? What is it about them you find challenging?

Teacher

We all have had teachers. Great teachers take responsibility for our learning and provide us with the information and knowledge that we require. They guide us to achievement and success.

Guru

A guru is different from a teacher. A guru helps us to unlearn all the stuff that we don't need and makes us responsible for our own inner growth.
A guru shows us the path towards freedom and self-sovereignty.

A guru can come in any shape or form… a difficult interaction, a horrible event, a painful break-up, a demanding relationship… a mean boss, an unpleasant neighbour…
A guru makes you aware of your inner resources and empowers your internal growth through self-learning.

Great teachers help us to learn about the world in order to boost our ego.
A great guru helps us to understand our own self in order to break our ego.

Think about: A person who turned out be a guru in your life. Think about what you learned.

Void

When we have an argument with someone close to us we feel hurt. Sometimes we try to cope with the aftermath of the argument by pretending nothing has happened.
We force ourselves to act normally. We try to void the feelings of emotional hurt. This avoidance and suppression is like burying our head in the sand.
Inside, we are still feeling horrible but we continue pretending everything is fine and what she/he said did not really affect anything and nothing has taken place.
In the long run such suppression or avoidance is damaging.

Validate

After an argument or a disagreement with someone who we are close to there is bound to be emotional hurt and pain. It is not good to pretend that nothing has happened. It is very important to acknowledge your emotions in that situation. Tell yourself or the other person:
'I am still upset and feeling very sad with what has happened and I am trying to resolve it in my head.'
By doing this we take away the need to blame or for everything to resolve instantly.
We also validate our emotions and remove the pressure to feel OK immediately.

Trying to void something that is already out there is quite difficult.
It is OK to feel a little hurt, angry, and sad or upset after an argument.

Be OK with your emotions after an argument, acknowledge them and let them pass.
Don't try to supress them or pretend nothing has happened.

Suggestion: Next time after an argument or when you are upset acknowledge your emotions and feelings, and name them.

Anger, hatred, jealousy, grief, rejection, shame, bitterness, disgust, rage, sadness, shock…?

Navigating

Some parents want to plan and direct the course of the lives of their children. They want to manage the exact way their children's lives pan out. They mean well but this is about their own plan.

Parents should remember that the children have their own unique map...

Nurturing

Nurturing is about providing the right environment for the growth and development of the children. It is not about control; it is about care, encouragement and unconditional love. It is not about planning the course of the life of the children but it is about providing support and guidance so that they can read their own map well.

Nurturing is not about giving a perfect life to your children; it means to teach them to find their own way of being in the imperfect world.

Children need to be nurtured not navigated.

Think about: Top three guidance lessons which you learned from your parents that you are thankful for.

It's you

'It's you' is about laying all the blame on the other person:
You said this... if only you had said...
You did that... if only you had not done that...
You made me do... if only you had not...
You are like this... if only you were...

It's me

Blame serves no purpose in a relationship.
The wisest truth is that it is only ever useful to look at what you could have done differently rather than waste time blaming things on the other person.
'It's me' is not about self-blame, it is about self-reflection.

Be aware of your own behaviour before you judge others.
Did you do everything right?

People of the world don't look at themselves, and so they blame one another.
Rumi

Think about: A situation where you blamed your partner/the other person. Just put their behaviour aside and ask yourself, 'What did I do that was not entirely right/correct in the situation?'

50/50

50/50 is about putting in half/half. I give half and you also have to give half.

Many modern-day relationships are often based on 'going Dutch'.

I pay my half of the bill and you pay your half.

It's good not to expect the other person to take care of your expenses but what's worse is when you don't want to share what you have with others.

Sticking rigidly to the 50/50 rule is a bit selfish and stingy. It means you can only give when the other person puts in their bit.

You can't bring only half of yourself to a relationship, and sharing of the expenses is about participating fully in the relationship, not just about splitting costs 50/50.

100/100

100/100 is about both people in the relationship giving their best shot.

This has nothing to do with money. It is about being there 100% for the other person. It's about bringing 100% effort to the relationship.

When you are with a person 100% then it is not just about equal contributions, it is about sharing whatever there is for the greater good and future of the relationship.

100/100 is the only way for a true relationship.
It is not about 50/50 calculation of the contributions.
You cannot leave 50% of yourself out of the relationship, you need to be there 100%.

In a relationship splitting the bills and costs in half is about sharing.
It is not about making sure the other person contributes same as you.

Think about: A couple who have a 100/100 relationship according to you. What is it you admire about them? Also try to have an insight into how they share their finances, bills etc.

Soulmate

Soulmate is a myth. Soulmates do not exist. Soul is an entity by itself and does not mate with anyone. Mating is only of the body, not of the soul.
No one has lived your life and they cannot go inside your head to know exactly how you see the world. Even two leaves from the same tree are not exactly the same so how can two people with different genders or even the same one be exactly alike.
Waiting for a soulmate who will understand you exactly the way you want them to and will see and experience the entire world exactly like you do is a fantasy.

Sure mate

Sure mate is a person who you respect and hold in high regard. Sure mate may not know your every single thought but they try their very best to understand what is important to you. They see the world with their own perspective, and although their perspective may be different from yours, they have the ability to respect yours.
Their views enhance the way you see the world and help you to grow.

Perfect ready-made soulmates may or may not appear out of the blue.
In the meantime true, selfless, unconditional friendships and love can always be cultivated.

The perfect soulmate does not exist.
Perfect moments with people we love do happen...

Exercise: Make two lists, one of unreal 'soulmate' expectations and the other of realistic sure mate virtues.

Yes but...

During discussions we often use the term 'Yes but...'
'Yes but...' is bit of an oxymoron. 'Yes' means to agree with something and 'but' means giving a reason to disagree with something.
When we don't have the courage to say a clear 'No', 'Yes but...' sometimes becomes a 'No' in disguise.
Have you noticed that we often say 'Yes but...' to our own selves internally more often than we say that to other people.

Yes and...

'Yes and...' shows clear agreement for someone's idea and it also shows added support to build on the presented idea.
'Yes and...' feels positive and collaborative. It does not mean that you agree with everything; it just means your first response is to be open with the intention to explore what has been suggested.

'Yes AND...' means saying yes to life circumstances and adding more positivity on the top.
'Yes BUT...' means sending a message of exclusion, limitation, denial and rejection into the universe.

Yes AND... is a mentality that allows you to explore and be more positive and open-minded.
Yes BUT... cuts conversations and keeps us stuck.

Exercise: Count how many times you say 'Yes but...' in a day.

Letting Go

We often think that moving on means letting go. Letting go is about the need to remove something or someone from our life completely.

Removing or getting rid of something, be it a person or our own emotion, is like throwing something away. Getting rid of something externally does not mean 'moving on'; it means being stuck at the same place but with the object or person removed from your sight.

Letting Be

Letting be is the power to truly move on. It means that there is no internal need for getting rid of or removing someone or something from your life externally. You can just let it or let them be, as they no longer have the ability to affect you internally.

Letting be means truly moving on yourself and letting others be...

Letting go is about discarding, letting be is about detaching.

The process of letting go of something should lead to letting be...
When you truly move on you can let others be.
Moving on means letting things be as they are and they don't affect you anymore...

Think of: Past situations that you are still trying to let go of in your head. Try to remove the pressure from your head and instead just let them be. Allow your heart to move on...

Apology

Apology means someone expresses sorrow for what has happened; it does not necessarily mean that they have actually accepted responsibility for what has happened.

Being Sorry

Being sorry is different from just offering an apology. Being sorry for something means having the courage to not only say it in words but also to follow it up with rectified actions.

An apology followed by the same behaviour means nothing.
Apologies can be just empty words.
Being sorry means new action or behaviour.

Saying sorry and meaning sorry are two very different things.
Being truly sorry is not about just words.
It is expressed by feelings and actions.

Think about: A time when someone said sorry to you but repeated the same mistake again. How did it make you feel?

Sad Endings

Endings can be sad and painful. Often when we wallow too long in the pain of something that is ending we forget that every ending is a new beginning for something else. It's up to us to either keep looking backwards or to face the future and look ahead.

Happy Beginnings

New beginnings can be scary and that is why we keep focusing on something that is ending or has ended. Beginnings may be scary at first but they bring new opportunities and new possibility of creating happy endings. It is better to keep the focus on the new beginnings and make them happy rather than keep feeling unhappy about the endings and make the new beginnings sad.

Life is full of endings and beginnings. It is in a constant flow.
Some things are ending whilst other things are beginning.
Night ends, dawn breaks and a new day begins.
Sad ending or happy beginning, it's a matter of your focus.

Forget about your last sad ending.
Start right now and think about making a new happy beginning.

Think about: A time when something ended in your life, a relationship, a job, a situation – how did you feel at the time? How did it all turn out later?

Work Engagement

Managing

In the workplace either we have managed others or others have managed us.
In everyday work situations, managing others means:
Monitoring others
Doing things right
Instructing
Talking to Staff
Giving Feedback
Team functionality
Detail of things

Leading

Leading in the workplace relates to creating clear vision for the common goal.
Leading means:
Empowering others
Doing the right thing
Inspiring
Talking with Staff
Giving Praise
Team building
Seeing the bigger picture

Managing and leading are both necessary in the work environment.
It is important to be aware of the difference so as to create the right balance.

Leadership has been glamorized perhaps a bit too much. Leading and managing are both important. Strong leaders need strong managers.

Idea: Identify a historical leader you admire. Read their biography and do some research on them. Write down a short paragraph about the qualities that you really admired about them.

Compromise

Compromise means meeting halfway. It means putting aside some of your own ideas in order to accommodate some of the ideas of the other person or party.
It is somewhat like a 50/50 split. When someone puts aside 50% of themselves and their vision, are they going to be happy? Can one put aside 50% of themselves?

Collaboration

Collaboration is about creating a partnership where no one has to put aside some part of who they are for the sake of agreement.
Collaboration means moving forward with the feeling that the best solution for all is about what is best of all.
Collaboration means that everyone involved brings 100% of who they are into the team.

Compromise is just about agreement.
Collaboration is much more powerful and dynamic. It is about uniting forces and creating synergy.

In a successful and happy team people go beyond compromise, they collaborate authentically.

Idea: Start a community project. Try to bring people from different parts together. Encourage them to collaborate authentically.

Clock

You are constantly checking the clock.
You have monthly, weekly, daily and hourly schedules.
You accomplish all your tasks by strict and successful time management.
You organize every single second of your time.
Yet, you have absolutely no clue where your life is headed...

Compass

Living your life by the compass means to know the direction and purpose of your life.
To know that your life is on the correct path. To feel that whatever you do on a daily basis has some purpose towards the aims of your life.
Living by the compass does not mean being careless about schedules and poor timekeeping; it means to understand the importance of the daily tasks and deeper value of the passing time in the big picture.

Are you living your life by the clock or the compass?
Are you so caught up in managing your minutes, hours, days that you are avoiding your entire life?

Your inner compass is important, perhaps more important than the clock in the office.
Feel your inner compass and don't let your life go by just looking at the office clock.

Suggestion: Look at your weekly schedule, really look at it. This is your life; are you happy with it?

Self Employed

Many people desire to be self-employed in order to do what they want to do and whenever they want to do it. In concept being self-employed sounds much better than scraping a living in some job that you are tied to with no freedom and have absolutely no interest in.

However, being self-employed in other words means you create a job for yourself. You do a job, but for yourself and not for someone else. This is great. However, many people who embark on this journey to self-employment soon realize that in order to remain self-employed they actually have to do not just their own job but also do the jobs of other people. They have to do the job of the secretary, the administrator, the office clerk, the tea lady plus their own job.

In reality this is much more work and also greater time commitment than their previous job.

The fantasy of self-employment is different from reality.

If you want to become self-employed just to work less, think again.

Business Owner

Being a business owner is different from just creating a job for yourself. Often people want to become business owners; in reality they end up giving themselves the job of a business manager.

Becoming a business owner comes with a certain attitude and philosophy. It is about creating something rather than just working at something. It is also not just about selling your product or skill. The business owner has a vision and this vision is beyond just making an income. It is about contributing towards the change of something, adding value to something or innovating something.

Wealth is generated as a by-product of the actualization of the vision.

Do you have a vision?

If your aim in becoming self-employed is just so you can work less and lie around on the beach, you better just reduce your hours in your current job.

Be aware of what the difference is between being self-employed, a business manager and a business owner.

I am not self-employed, I run a business.
A business built on the blood and tears of my innermost thoughts and desires.
Every time my soul cries like a banshee, something new emerges.
This isn't merely employment.
This is every single breath feeling a crazy creative, meaningful moment.
Unknown

Think about: People are suited to different things. Some to employment and some to business. Examine what suits you best and why.

No Stress

Some strain or struggle is a part of life. It happens to all of us time to time. We have all felt it and we also know that there will indeed be some situation in the future that will bring us some tension or strain.
This is bound to happen.
To hope that there won't ever be any sort of pressure, strain or tension, worry, anxiety at all about anything at all ever in life or your job is a bit unrealistic.
No matter how fantastic we become at managing life, people, situations, family, health or job it is inevitable that at some point some situation or some people will cause us some sort of stress.
'No stress' is not a possibility.

Know Stress

Recognizing the symptoms of your own stress is important.
To have the awareness of your state and knowing how stress feels is a very useful thing.
When you notice that you are stressed and you have the ability to recognize it you can then also take some steps to manage it. If you are not aware that it's you who is stressed and instead keep blaming other people… then in that state more and more things or people will wind you up. The more wound up you become, the more anxious you will feel and then this is likely to become a vicious circle.
Knowing stress is good. Being aware of your stress and understanding how to manage it is important.

Once you know that you are stressed you can do something about it.
The problem is that when people don't recognize their own stress then they either reach a burnout or they start offloading their stress on to other people.
To recognize and manage your own stress is an important skill.

Do you know 'stressed' spelled backwards is 'desserts'… yummy! When you are stressed think of things that make you feel relaxed.

Exercise: Think of three songs that make you feel good. Remember these when you feel stressed. Let them play in your mind.

Monetary Wealth

Financial gain is the purpose of businesses.

The aim of a business venture is to have profit. Profit is what is left in monetary terms after deducting the investment and expenditures.

Generally the success of a business is related to the monitory wealth it generates.

Generating and creating wealth is what drives most people in the first place to start their own businesses.

Moral Wealth

There is also something else, other than the monetary gain in a business setting. This is moral wealth.

Inequality, corruption, fraud, exploitation are all losses; they deplete the moral wealth of the business.

A business generates moral wealth by goodwill, integrity, generosity, and fairness.

Don't just focus on acquiring monitory wealth; also grow your moral wealth.

A business can generate lots of financial profits but unless it is also
creating moral wealth it is not a completely successful business.

Exercise: List 10 things that you think can generate moral wealth for a business.

Passive Income

Quite a lot of people dream of passive income. They fantasize about getting regular income without them having to do any effort for it.

In lay terms passive income is derived from some venture that one is not actively or directly involved in.

Passive income is the ultimate fantasy. Who wouldn't want income coming in regularly without having to do anything at all...

Ironically, quite a lot of people are already earning passive income without their knowledge. They just turn up to their job every day, but they are reluctant to put in any real effort. They just passively do their required tasks but are not 100% into it and do nothing actively to contribute to their work environment or people around them...

They are earning a 'passive' income, while they are 'actively' wasting their life!

Automated Income

Unlike the popular belief regarding automated income it does not happen automatically at all. It requires a lot of foresight, planning and setting systems in place. These then thereafter generate a flow of income regularly.

Many companies are touting courses, seminars and workshops that profess that you can generate passive and automated income effortlessly. All you have to do is pay for the course and they will show you the tricks.

Before paying for any such activity, one must examine what attracts you to passive and automated income.

If it is just about having it easy and getting something by doing nothing, then the only automated income that will be generated will be for the company that has sold you that course.

Automated income is definitely not about having it easy or about 'not working'.

It is about making your ideas work for you creatively by putting in a lot of work and planning.

Passive income and automated income are preceded by hard work and dedication.
There is nothing passive or automated about them.

Suggestion: Look up the self-made millionaires you admire. Research their lives; find out what difficulties and hardships they went through to get where they are now.

Ideas

Many success stories are based on brilliant ideas and ideas there are many.

In the harsh reality of the business world nobody really cares about your idea unless it becomes something real.

It may appear that many business successes have occurred because of one amazing idea and nothing else. This is, however, far from the truth; anyone who has had business success knows that success does not come just from the idea itself but loads of other stuff.

Implementation

Implementation is all about bringing the idea from your inside world to the outside world. It is about making your idea real.

Making it real involves action and execution and loads of hard work.

An idea by itself will do nothing:
Idea + Action + Determination = Success

Don't stop thinking or creating new ideas, they are valuable. However, without execution they just remain thoughts in our heads.
Everyone has around 80,000 thoughts per day.

Exercise: Think about one small idea that you have had for years. List just five actions related to it. Start with action number one – just do it!

Turnover

In the business context this is the money that flows in and out of the business. Some money comes in, some money goes out. This is the turnover of the business.

The total sum of all the monetary activity can look impressive on a spreadsheet. A company can have a great turnover, but in reality it may not be actually making much profit at all…

So just like this, some people may be doing a lot of stuff in their life. Perhaps they are involved in many social activities, sports, events, functions, holidays etc., etc. Their life may look amazing from the outside, but they still don't feel right. They feel something is missing. They seem to be doing loads of things but are they achieving nothing internally.

Profit

Profit refers to the surplus of money you have after you have paid your expenses.

A business needs profits to be successful.

Likewise in life it's not just the activities, job, house, holidays etc. that make a successful life; it's what's left after all that. If the experiences and activities and involvements give a feeling of an amazing and fulfilled life, then you are making a profit. If after all the involvements and lifestyle you still have a lack inside and feel that something is missing, then you are not making any profit in your life.

Fundamental questions:
Is your business making any profit?
Is your life fulfilled?

Businesses like to flaunt their turnover but often keep quiet about their real profits.

Likewise many people often brag a lot about their lifestyle, when they don't really have anything to say about their true happiness.

Idea: Select a person you know as a role model who you think has a profitable business/fulfilled life. Spend some time with them just generally chatting about their business/life. From the conversation identify what particular strengths they have and how did they use those strengths to get to where they are now.

Whirlwind

In business or work environments we all experience some stress time to time.
Stress can soon build up and cause anxiety. This can have a negative effect on the rest of the life and overall well-being.
Stress is a barometer that indicates something is not quite right.
If you are lying awake at night thinking about deadlines and feel completely immobilized by the stress then it's time to examine things at a deeper level.
It can either be your ability to manage your own stress or your inability to say no to unwarranted demands or your suitability for the job.
Stress is like a whirlwind, it can take us down.

Propeller

Some pressure at work is good, it makes us diligent. If there is no pressure at all it can lead to boredom. It is good to recognize good pressure and use it to propel us to do better at our job.
Think of pressure as the propeller on a plane or a ship. It creates the right type of tension and challenge to boost a forward movement.
For example a deadline can create anxiety, but if it is seen as something that is pulling you forward then it becomes a positive thing.

It is important to know the difference between stress and pressure in order to manage them well.
Some pressure is good, it stimulates us to do the things we need to do.
Unmanaged pressure can develop into stress and stress is not good.

Diamonds are formed under pressure. Without pressure there would be no diamonds.

Exercise: Identify the things that make you stressed at work. List them down and also write down your own strategies to deal with them.

Problem Talk

Problems are part of life and also part of any work environment.
Problem talk simply means focusing on the problem and asking these questions:
What went wrong?
Why did it happen?
Who is to be blamed?
Sometimes such analysis is indeed important.
It is important to also be aware that sometimes focusing too much on the problem amplifies the perception of the problem itself. This can actually make the people involved unhappy and less keen to actually solve the problem. This can also affect the atmosphere of the organization and make it more negative.

Solution Talk

For most problems there are solutions and solution talk simply means focusing on the solution and not the problem.
How can we solve this?
What resources are available?
What is working and how we can make that even better?
What would be the first step to take?
Which strengths do we have collectively to take this forward?
Solution talk is just a way to take the focus away from the problem and concentrate on moving forward.

Focusing on the problem can keep us stuck, and at times we actually miss seeing the new path.
Sometimes people can get so tangled in the problem that this can result in a downward spiral making the problem even worse.

Good managers and leaders focus on solving the problem and not just the problem itself.
Office gossip on the other hand indulges in just problem talk and not the solution.

Idea: Next time there is a problem at work, ask all the related team members to each write a solution based on the strengths and resources available. Put all of the suggestions in a jar; label it the 'Solutions Jar'. Organize a meeting. Ask each member to pick out a solution from the jar and read it aloud. Ask everyone to discuss what works about that particular solution. In the end create an amalgamated solution from all the positive suggestions.

Feedback

Feedback is evaluation of the work done by an employee related on their past performance. The main purpose is to enhance the productivity or improve their work in the future. More often than not it usually ends up as a list of things that the person didn't do correctly and what they should have done differently instead. It can sound critical and negative. Most of the people take feedback too personally and become defensive about it. Feedback is often something employees do not look forward to receiving.

Feedforward

Feedforward approach is suggestions about the future as opposed to corrections of mistakes in the past.
It is far easier for most people to take suggestions than listen to their mistakes of the past. Feedforward is less personal and far more dynamic and positive.
It is also far more productive to make suggestions to enable people to do new things than going over what they have been doing incorrectly.

Is giving Feedback to your staff fun? If not, why not change it to Feedforward!

What is the point of any feedback if doesn't change anything in the future?
Better to feedforward instead.

Exercise: Create feedforward reviews at work instead of feedback reviews.

Action Faking

Action faking has actually become a part of the modern-day hectic lifestyle.
Action faking is doing lots of things, but not the task itself. You can spend days to buy yourself the latest exercising gear. You can spend hours online researching which are the best running shoes to buy. You can spend even more hours writing your weekly timetable to incorporate exercise time in your busy schedule… you can read books about the benefits of regular exercise or which type of yoga will suit you… you can do all this, but unless you actually exercise for an hour – with or without the appropriate gym gear – the aim is not achieved.
All the preparations are just Action Faking.

Action Taking

Action taking is simply – doing the actual task!
Buying the running shoes does not mean exercise.
Putting on the running shoes and sitting around the house does not mean exercise.
Becoming a member at the gym does not mean exercise.
Watching YouTube exercise videos does not mean exercise.
Going for a run in the park for an hour – that's exercise.
Doing yoga for an hour – that's exercise.
Action taking is straightforward; it's about – just doing it!

Are you an action faker or an action taker?
Do you busy yourself with doing loads of stuff in order to avoid doing what actually needs to be done?

Action taking is simple. It's about just doing it!
Action faking is complicated. It involves lots of planning and lots more time and effort.

Think about: Which activity are you action faking? Write a date and time in your diary to actually start doing it.

Tension

When we are doing something our focus can wander from just doing the task to random worries about it… the outcome, what others think, what will happen next, will others do it better etc., etc. All this needless worry brings tension.

Attention

Being attentive towards what we are doing is a good thing. Attention means to keep focus on the task rather than start worrying about it.
It's the focus 'at' something that keeps us tension free.

Creating tension and paying attention towards something are two different things.

Attention is good; tension is not. Keep the attention 'at' something.
It's when you remove the 'at' from attention, it becomes tension.

Suggestion: Monitor your distractions such as phone, TV, and Internet while focusing on a particular task. Have breaks but do not let distractions interject random worries, and just keep your attention on the task.

Power

Power comes from the authority of the post and is attached to it. When the post ends the power also goes away.

Influence

Influence comes from the person; it is not tied to the title or the post.
An influential person is respected by others through their own will and not as an obligation towards their authority.

Someone who is influential is persuasive naturally.
They don't have to push or coax other people into doing or following something.
Good leaders become influential as they themselves follow what they say rather than use their authority to persuade people.
Influence creates an impact on someone's character; power on the other hand just affects the job or task.

You need Power only when you want to do something harmful otherwise Love is enough to get everything done.
Charlie Chaplin

Think about: Someone who has had a positive influence in your life. List the qualities that they have which you admire.

Monitoring

Monitoring your team is about checking whether they are following the given instructions.
Monitoring is about making the staff do their required work.

Motivating

Motivating your team is about making the team feel inspired to do what they need to do.
Motivating the team is about getting the staff to enjoy the work that they do.

When staff feel motivated, then they don't need monitoring. Monitoring is needed when staff are demotivated and have no willingness or desire to do their job.

Motivating someone means that they do what needs to be done willingly.
Monitoring someone means to check that they do what needs to be done correctly.
Often when there is no willingness, there are more errors.

Idea: Write down your three favourite motivational quotes and stick each one in a different place. Examples: Kitchen drawer, closet, bathroom mirror, work drawer, first page of the diary, screen saver...

Unconsciously Incompetent

It's good to reflect at your own job competence from time to time.
What skills are you lacking in relation to your job?
What do you need to improve?
An Unconsciously Incompetent person is someone who is not good at their job and has no awareness about it.
Not always but quite a lot of the times, an Unconsciously Incompetent person is in the wrong job.

Consciously Competent

When you know what you need to do and you have a good understanding of how to do it and you also have the awareness of what you need to improve you are Consciously Competent.
A Consciously Competent person is skilled in what they do and this comes with self-enquiry and reflection of one's own strengths and weaknesses.

Take responsibility for yourself; don't be unconsciously incompetent.
Find out what you need to know and then learn it and try to do it.

An unconsciously incompetent person is a burden to the team, whereas a consciously competent person is an asset.

Exercise: Do a self-assessment of your competence in relation to your job. Which areas do you think you need to develop more?

Under Control

When staff is kept too much 'under control' businesses weaken.
Too much control stifles the staff and their creativity, and the business stagnates.

In Control

Giving staff autonomy and letting them be 'in control' of their own roles develops and grows the business.
Businesses flourish when staff are made independent and empowered.

Allowing and encouraging people to be 'in control' of their role and responsibility makes them more motivated and empowered.

Good leadership is not about controlling people, it's about empowering them to discern well and let them be in control of their own path.

Idea: Declare a 'self-leadership' day at work for the roles that are usually required to be monitored closely. Allow these people to be totally 'in control' of their own day. Arrange a follow-up group meeting to talk about their learning experiences.

Activity

Activity is shuffling papers in order to look busy at work. It means doing things that keep you occupied but these are not getting you anywhere near your objectives.

Busy bees are always busy, they are always doing something. They appear very active… but what are they doing?

Productivity

Productivity means being engaged in tasks that move you forward towards your goals. Productivity does not always mean being busy. Sometimes productivity may mean sitting quietly for some time and mindfully planning things in relation to your goal.

Someone who is always active is perceived more efficient than someone who is perhaps not so busy.

It is important to remember that 'busy busy' does not always mean achievement.

Activity that is useless sucks up a lot of time, and that can be quite damaging especially for entrepreneurs and small businesses.

Activity can be doing something that doesn't need to be done in the first place.

On the other hand, productivity can mean doing nothing at all.

Think about: All the activities that waste time (some phone calls, some emails, various meetings, social media…). What steps can you take to reduce time wastage?

Wanterprenuer

Wanterprenuer is someone who wants to be an entrepreneur. They think they 'know how' to do business but in actual reality they are forever engaged in things that appear to be business but are not actual business.

They spend too much time on developing unique ideas, making logos, styling business cards, doing endless market research, attending numerous networking events… daydreaming endlessly about the lifestyles of successful businesspeople…

Entrepreneur

Entrepreneur is someone who starts their own business. Business is about making money.

Entrepreneur does not have to have the best or the most original idea as long as the idea is put into a business activity and makes real money.

You are not really an entrepreneur until your business has made real money.

Unless your idea has made some real money…
It might be an innovative experiment, but it's not a business yet.

Wanterprenuers get lost in the thick of thin things.
It's OK to start off as a Wanterprenuer but it's good to develop the clarity and objectivity of a real entrepreneur.

Think about: Three things that a Wanterprenuer does not do that successful entrepreneurs do…

Procrastination

We all know procrastination very well, it's when we keep putting off important things… this causes useless delay. More often than not, the real reason behind procrastination is lack of real desire to do something.

Postponing

Postponing is about making a conscious decision to change the deadline of something in an informed way. It is about changing your priorities in relation to what is happening right now. Like, perhaps in an emergency.

Procrastination happens when you are not being true to your objectives and yourself.

Only put off until tomorrow what you are willing to die having left undone.
Pablo Picasso

Ask yourself: About the activity that you have been procrastinating over for a long time. Examine the activity and ask yourself, 'What are the reasons behind the constant procrastination?'

Inter-personal Conflict

Interpersonal conflict can and does happen at work when people participating in a task see things differently.
Conflict can be demotivating and draining for all involved. In a conflicting situation it is very important to remember everyone sees things differently and no two people are exactly the same. It is also important to keep an open mind and for both parties to really try and understand each other's point of view first, before trying to explain their own.

Intrapersonal Conflict

Intrapersonal conflict is the conflict with oneself when internal values don't match the external activities. Sometimes people are not aware that this is going on in their head. They become unhappy with what they are doing not knowing why. They feel demotivated and frustrated.
Intrapersonal conflict can arise when you neglect yourself and don't spend time clarifying your own wants and wishes. It is important to develop good communication skills with yourself. Observe how you talk to yourself... Do you have an inner critic that constantly criticizes what you are doing? Be kind to yourself and put time aside every day to check with yourself if you are feeling and doing OK.

Conflict is natural, as people are different and often have different points of view.
In today's work environment there are many techniques and mechanisms to resolve Inter-personal Conflict.
It is Intrapersonal Conflict in the work environment that is often not recognized.

When someone's life aims do not match their job it brings real unhappiness and demotivation.
Managers and supervisors need the skill not only to recognize this but also the ability to provide support through it.

Suggestion: Next time when you are in a conflict with someone, tell yourself that you will first give it your best shot to try to understand the views of the other person before you try to explain yours.

Doing Things Right

Doing things right is about doing things the best way possible. The quickest, the cheapest, the easiest etc.
It is good to do things the best way possible, however, sometimes we can get awfully preoccupied by doing everything in the most perfect way possible.
It is important to keep in mind doing things perfectly does not mean what is being done is the best thing to do in the first place.
A robber can execute the robbery in a perfect way.

Doing the Right Thing

Doing the right thing is the ability to achieve the right goal in the end.
It basically means doing things to get the right job done.
It also means doing what is correct over what is the correct procedure.
In a long queue to see the doctor it's OK to let an elderly frail patient jump the queue...

Before doing anything it is good to examine whether it's the right thing to do in the first place.

Happiness and personal fulfilment are the natural consequences of doing the right thing.
Epictetus

Think about: Something you did perfectly yet in the end it was not the right thing to do. What would have been the correct thing to do instead?

Conflict Management

When two people at work or two parties are in strong disagreement it causes a lose-lose situation where no one gains and everyone loses. Companies usually dread such situations as they waste a lot of time and resources. Most organizations have some sort of conflict management strategies in place already.

Facilitating Communication

Facilitating communication is about making the understanding between people and groups better. This is a regular ongoing process and does not just take place when there is conflict. Facilitating good communication means encouraging good listening and mutual respect between people regularly.

Why wait until there is a conflict? Why not put some good practices in place that reduce the actual chance of conflict? This can be done by cultivating an atmosphere of mutual respect.

In many ways, effective communication begins with mutual respect, communication that inspires, encourages, or instructs others to do their best.
Zig Ziglar

Suggestion: Try this 'Strengths spotting exercise' at work. Ask colleagues to spot each other's strengths and write them on a chart called 'Strengths Tree'. This puts the focus on qualities rather than differences.

Shifting Responsibility

Shifting responsibility is making someone else accountable for your job. Some people can give their tasks to other people and get them to do their job but still take the credit for it if things go right, and if things don't go right they blame others. Shifting responsibility is basically about getting others to do your work for you.

Delegating

Delegating is entrusting someone to do some of your tasks with full awareness that you still hold the eventual responsibility if things don't go right.
However, when the work is completed well then it is also your responsibility to ensure the one who did the task gets the credit they deserve. The aim of delegation is to empower others.

When you delegate do it with the right intention.

Delegation is more than just making your own load light.
It is to do with the right intention.
It is about empowering, training and encouraging others.

Exercise: List all the tasks you would like to delegate to someone. Set a good intention for each task.

What's not working?

Continuous focus on what is not working keeps an organization stuck in repair mode.

If all the questions that are asked are about what does not work then all the answers that are received will also be about what is not working right. The focus then forever remains on that which does not work.

This sabotages progress.

What's working?

What's working is focusing on the positive aspects of what is actually going right. This is about looking at strengths and enhancing them further.

When the organization becomes stronger the potential for problems is less.

Focusing on what is working positively moves the organization forward.

Appreciative enquiry is the art and practice of asking questions that strengthen an organization.

Asking questions about what is working rather than continually enquiring about the problems.

If I had an hour to solve a problem and my life depended on the solution, I would spend the first 55 minutes determining the proper question to ask, for once I know the proper question, I could solve the problem in less than five minutes.

Albert Einstein

Exercise: Write a short email mentioning one thing that is going well and send it to one person in the team and ask that person to add another thing that is going well and forward it to another, so on and so forth… then depending on the size of the team read all the comments in a group meeting.

Networking

Networking means getting the contact details of as many people as possible, thinking that some of these contacts may turn out to be useful in some way in the future. People can end up with hundreds of business cards just after one big networking event.

Such networking can sometimes give a false sense of connection and it can also turn out to be a bit too much about your own agenda.

Meeting People

Meeting people is just about meeting people. It is about getting to know different people and what they do and what their interests are...

It is not about thinking how useful a certain contact may or may not be to you in the future. It is just about making real connections with people.

Cultivate relationships, do not just collect them.
Pursuing connections just to gain something for yourself is a bit selfish.
Think how useful you could be for the other person.

You can take yourself to as many networking events as you want. Contacts alone do not create good business, good relationships do.

Do: Next time you are at a social function, don't try to network, just try to meet people.

Earning Money

Earning money is about having the funds to sustain yourself in the material world. You earn money so you can buy the things you want in this world. Earning money means having money in your bank account. For some people the primary aim of life is to earn loads of money and build a huge bank account.

Earning Blessings

Earning blessings is about your karmic account.
It is about doing good to others. Providing for the needy, nurturing the sick, caring for the elderly…
You earn blessings to create a good karmic account for yourself.
For some people the primary goal of their life is to cultivate a good karmic account.

A good karmic account means you have loads of spiritual wealth. You might have loads of money in your big bank account, but unless you also have some spiritual wealth the money won't do anything for you.

Earning money is not enough for a happy life. One must also earn blessings.

Think about: You know exactly how much you earned last month; if you can't remember you can just check your bank account. Do you know exactly how many blessings you earned last month? Think about all the good and meaningful things you did for others last month.
Don't just look at your back account – also check your karmic account time to time…

Priority

Sometimes decisions can be confusing and we don't know what to choose.
We think of priorities in relation to making decisions.
In life priorities are not just about expensive or cheap, near or far, less or more etc.
These are just about the logistics of everyday life.
Real priorities are about who we are as a human being and our core values.

Option

With everyday stuff it is much easier to view decisions as options in order not to be paralyzed by availability of alternatives.
It's better to say to yourself, 'Well these are the options available to me. Different options just bring different things. Whatever I choose I know it will be good for now. I also know nothing stays the same forever. I am sure other options will be available to me at a different stage.'
With this way choosing and decision-making become easier and lighter.

Priorities are about what's important and what's high on the list.
Options are not higher or lower, they are just different possibilities.
Most everyday stuff is just about different options.
Different options bring different things and experiences.

Priorities are about your big stuff, who you are and your values. Once you have that sorted, those everyday decisions are just your options.

Think about: What are your top three priorities in life?

Monday Moaning

Do you moan about Monday mornings?
Do you think, 'Oh no, it's Monday again!' Do you get a sinking feeling on Sunday night and an elated feeling on Friday afternoon? Do you hate Mondays?

Monday Morning

Do Monday mornings bring you enthusiasm for the week ahead?
Do you feel excited as the new week starts and you say, 'Yes, it's Monday!'
Do you love Mondays?

Are you living your entire life just for that Friday feeling?
Life should not just be what happens between Friday evening until Monday morning.
Life is every single breath we take, be it Friday or Monday.
Each day should be loved like a gift.

Love Mondays.
Mondays means it's time to make your dreams a reality.

Do: Observe your feelings on Monday morning. What do you feel – enthusiasm, boredom, excitement, dullness, fear, joy...?

Soul and Meaning

Reacting

Many people go through their entire life only ever reacting to situations and circumstances.
Reacting means the control lies with the situation or the other person and not with us.
For example: When we get angry, we say he/she 'made me' angry.
Getting angry because of someone or something on the outside means you are just reacting to that situation and have no control over your own behaviour or thoughts.
It means you are not exercising your choice. You are just being controlled by what's external.
It is like letting someone else control the steering wheel of the car you are driving.

Responding

When you respond to something it means you choose the way you will act or behave towards the situation rather than allowing the external factors or the situation to influence your thoughts or behaviour automatically.
Example: When someone shouts at you, you shout back at them immediately and you say he/she shouted at me and 'made me' shout back.
Nobody can make you do anything, the choice is yours.
So when someone shouts at you, instead of shouting back you can consciously choose your response.
Responding is basically choosing the best thing to do in the moment rather than the situation 'making' you do something.

It is important to become aware of the choice that exists between stimulus and our response.
The difference between reacting and responding is the awareness of choice.
Reacting means acting impulsively without awareness.
Responding means choosing to do the best possible thing within that moment.

Between stimulus and response there is a space. In that space is our power to choose our response.
In our response lies our growth and our freedom.
Viktor Frankl

Exercise: During a conversation today become fully aware of what you say and how you say it. Choose what you will say before replying. Choose the tone of your voice and also your facial expressions. After the conversation reflect on your responses.

Role Consciousness

Role consciousness means attaching yourself to your roles. You play many roles through life. Your roles are your gender, job title, ethnicity, nationality, age, sexuality etc., etc.
In one day alone, you play many roles. In the morning you are a mother, at work you are a manager, in a clinic you are a patient, in the car you are the driver, in the evening you are a wife...
When you attach yourself unconsciously to your roles, you end up thinking you are just the roles you play.

Soul Consciousness

Soul consciousness means knowing that all the titles and labels that identify you are only your external roles. You exist despite those. Those roles are only temporary and forever changing. A student may later become a teacher. An employee may become an employer. A son might become a father...
The soul does not change, it is what's there under the layers of all the external roles.
The responsibilities of the roles change with them. The qualities of the soul are permanent and eternal.
A student can be a 'kind' student and later become a 'kind' teacher. The employee can be an 'honest' employee and can later be an 'honest' employer.

We play many roles in this world just like an actor that plays many parts in various plays.
It is important to remember that you are not just your roles.
You are what you give through those roles.
If you give love, peace, happiness – you are love, peace and happiness.

Whatever role you play in any given moment, your true identity is your soul.

Your soul gives quality to your roles.

Exercise: Write down all the things that identify you externally (ethnicity, gender...) and list all the roles you play in a typical day (job, relationships...). Also make a list of your soul qualities. Visualize using your soul qualities in each of your roles.

Self-centred

A self-centred person is simply a selfish person who lacks consideration for other people. He/she is only capable of focusing on his/her own pleasure and interests.
Although self-centred people are preoccupied with their selfish interests, in reality they do not have that much awareness of their own real internal needs. They are forever looking to gain something from the outside in order to make them OK on the inside.

Being Centred

Being centred is the inner state of equanimity. A centred person knows that in order to interact with the ever-changing external world inner stability is required.
Being centred means to be aware of your state of mind and in control of your responses, and being fully present in the moment.
Being centred also means being aligned with your purpose and being at peace with the things around you.

A self-centred person has a feeling of emptiness inside, and no matter what they indulge in that feeling never goes away. This empty feeling comes from the lack of inner alignment.

Being centred means to be stable and aligned inside. Self-centred on the other hand means to be disconnected on the inside, so that one makes 'self' the centre of everything on the outside.

Think about: A time when you were selfish. What was the situation? How would you be different now in the same situation?

Outside-in

Outside-in means letting everything that is on the outside have an influence over how you feel inside.
For example: people, politics, media, partner, weather, possessions...
- He said/she said -> made me angry.
- It's raining -> I am annoyed.
- I lost my phone ->I am very sad.

Inside-out

Inside-out means being OK and peaceful inside so that you can respond to everything on the outside appropriately.
Inside-out means to have the qualities within to take care of the outside.
For example: peace, love, tranquillity, acceptance, understanding...
- I understand why he said/she said ->I don't feel upset.
- I am going to read as it is raining ->I love reading.
- I have a new phone as I lost the old one -> things come and go.

It is easier living from inside-out as we can control and influence our own selves, but it is not possible to control everything and everyone on the outside.
Living from outside-in is quite difficult and brings lots of disappointments.

Your vision will become clear only when you can look into your own heart.
Who looks outside dreams; who looks inside awakes.
Carl Jung

Suggestion: Find some alone time and sit quietly and comfortably, and listen to a guided meditation. Put aside all worries for few minutes and focus on creating a feeling of tranquillity and peace inside. Take this inner feeling of tranquillity and peace to your outside world...

Meaning of Life

What is the meaning of life?
Why does life exist?
These are big questions...
Quite overwhelming!
Enough wise men have pondered over these questions and there are loads of existential philosophies.
There are no right or wrong answers.

Meaning in Life

Whatever the meaning of life, one thing is simple – that we all have different lives and perhaps we all need to create meaning in our own life individually.
For some –
- life is a mystery that needs to be solved.
- life is a game and that has to be won.
- life is a story that needs to be told.
- life is a lesson that has to be learned.

So on...

Why get lost with the big questions...
Why not simplify this dilemma and just create your own meaning...
We might not be able to prove the meaning of life but we can create meaning in our life by choosing to do the things that matter to us.

Bring meaning in your life by doing what really matters to you. What really matters to you is the meaning of your life.

Think: What brings meaning in your life? There are no right or wrong answers. Write down everything that comes to your mind.

Lesson

Lesson is the wisdom we acquire when we go through some tough experiences in life. We go through many experiences in life but not all experiences end up as lessons learned. Some lessons still need to sink in, that is why some situations or difficulties keep reappearing.

Test

In life tests appear in the form of difficulties and problems. How well we do in the test depends on the qualities we have acquired through our previous learning.
Whatever we can't deal with... is an indicator of what we still need to learn.
Tests are great revealers of our spiritual score.

Appreciate all the tests that life offers as these reveal your spiritual score.

In school you first have the lesson and then you are tested on it. In life you get the test first, so that you can learn a lesson from it.
Anonymous

Think about: A tough experience you went through. Reflect upon what you learned from that experience.

Mind-full

Have you ever felt that your mind is so full with things that you fail to notice what is happening around you?
It is like when you go on a train journey and when you get to your destination you remember nothing about the journey at all…
Mind can be full all the time with loads of thoughts about past, present, future…
Some thoughts are necessary, useful and positive.
Most thoughts are unnecessary, useless and negative.
A full mind cannot pay attention to the present, as it is lost in the clutter of all sorts of thoughts.

Mindful

Mindfulness means having full awareness of the present moment.
It means you have full awareness of yourself and whatever is happening right now. Your mind is not wandering off to some past events or feelings. You are not thinking about some future event like the weekend, a holiday…
It is about paying full attention to 'right here, right now'.
Mindfulness is about filtering the unnecessary, useless and negative thoughts and only having the thoughts that are useful and positive for the present moment.
When the mind is 'not full' it participates fully and positively with what is happening in the present moment.

'Now' is a gift which is why it is called the Present.
When the mind is too full, it has no space to receive the gift of the present moment.
When you free some space in your mind, then you can receive the Present.

Mindfulness is simply being aware of what is happening right now without wishing it were different; enjoying the pleasant without holding on when it changes (which it will); being with the unpleasant without fearing it will always be this way (which it won't).

James Baraz

Exercise: Take a moment right now to try this. Set five minutes on your clock. Just observe what's around you, hear the sounds, feel how and where you are sitting, notice your breathing. Observe your thoughts, don't fight them just observe them quietly. Become fully present.

Excitement

When we buy something new like a new car or we meet a new love interest... we feel very excited and we confuse this with happiness.
Excitement comes from the outside. It is dependent on something or someone.
It is a momentary thrill, buzz...
It is about novelty, newness, and as soon as the novelty diminishes the excitement also fades.

Happiness

Happiness is a feeling of deep contentment that comes from inside of you.
To be happy you don't need to have the 'right conditions', you can be happy regardless of any situation or person.
Happiness is not about new or old as it is inside of us...
Sometimes we just forget that it's there.

We often confuse happiness with excitement.
They both come and go in life but they are both quite different.
It is good to be able to distinguish between them and know each of them for what they are.
So that when excitement fades, we don't get upset or dissatisfied with the person or the object.

Many people think excitement is happiness... but when you are excited you are not peaceful.
True happiness is based on peace.
Thich Nhat Hanh

Think about: A time when you felt excited about something or someone, and a time when you felt true happiness. Compare the two feelings. How are they different?

Growing Old

Growing old means you become more and more fixed in the way you do things.
It means the different ways others do things bothers you more and more. It means you cannot easily adapt to new things, and can get irritated easily with others.
Growing old relates to age.
Aging is inevitable.

Growing Up

Growing up is a virtue that has to be acquired.
Growing up means you learn to understand 'your way' is not the 'only' correct way; you start to appreciate others and their different ways.
It means you become more tolerant and accepting. Little things do not irritate or bother you as much.
Growing up relates to wisdom.
Wisdom is acquired through awareness.

Everybody grows old with age, not everyone grows up according to his or her age.

Growing old is when you feel you are losing your physical beauty. Growing up is when you know you are acquiring inner beauty.

Think about: How old are you? What have you learned to accept over the years? What things irritated you years ago but don't irritate you any more... What things are you grown-up about now?

Medication

We take daily vitamin pills to keep the body healthy.
We may even be taking specific medication if our body is not well and it needs to get better.
The vitamins or the medicine gives the body the necessary nutrients to make it healthy and strong or get better.

Meditation

Meditation is like the daily vitamins for inner well-being.
It's like the daily nutrients for the soul.
Meditation keeps the mind healthy and strong. It gives the mind the dose of daily stability and peace.

Think of meditation as your daily dose of vitamins.
It keeps your mind healthy and gives it the necessary nutrients.
Just like vitamins or medication is taken with food, meditation is taken with silence.

Meditation is daily nutrition for the soul and well-being.
Like vitamins don't replace food for the body, medication does not replace meditation for complete well-being.

Exercise: Every morning put aside ten minutes for daily meditation. If you are not familiar with silent meditation, listen to guided meditation commentary.

Nil Mind

It is not possible to empty the mind. The mind can never be nil. Many people think that meditation happens when we have no thoughts. They sit in front of the candle and try to nil the mind. The mind doesn't become nil.
Then they feel meditation is not possible for them.

Still Mind

Still mind just observes and does not participate. It does not jump from past to future. It is focused on the present. It does not fall prey to random and negative thoughts.
It observes the thoughts and does not get involved emotionally with them.
It remains still and calm.

The mind is like an active child; it can become still but it cannot become nil.
Instead of trying to banish all thoughts, it is far easier to try to become calm and let the mind concentrate on thinking positive thoughts.

When the mind is still, then the truth gets her chance to be heard in the purity of silence.
Sri Aurobindo

Do: Practise three minutes of silence and stillness right now. Close your eyes and just observe your thoughts. Let them appear on a screen like you are watching a film. Observe the quality of your thoughts... Are they useful, random, wasteful, negative, positive...?

Absorbing

Absorbing means you get emotionally involved with everything that is happening around you. You let it affect the state of your mind. You easily get upset, irritated, sad and angry with things on the outside.

Observing

Observing means you have a clear view and understanding of the things that are happening around you but you do not give them power. You do not let them affect the inner balanced state of your mind. You remain in good view of them but you only participate when it is right and necessary.

In life it is good to learn how to be a skilled observer.
An observer knows when it is good to get involved and when to stay detached.
An absorber soaks up all energies without filtering the negative and has little control over his emotions.

An observer has a good view of what is happening.
An absorber is that close soaking up things that he cannot see the whole picture.
Observing is not about playing safe by not getting involved.
It is about knowing when is the right time to stay detached and when to get involved.

Exercise: For some time try to remain in an 'observer mode'; only get involved when it is necessary and important. This applies not only with what is happening around you but also with what is going on inside of you...

Shelf Development

Shelf development means buying the books, going to the talks, watching inspirational videos, going on retreats, listening to inspiring lectures, reading motivating articles, collecting encouraging quotes… BUT failing to practise all that you have learned.

Self-Development

Real self-development is about practice.

Practice is not just about reading or watching the right stuff. It means doing what you have learned and applying the learning in all your interactions.

Shelf-development is collection.
Self-development is application.
The journey from shelf development to self-development can be a lifetime.

Shelf development is about collecting and adding things or experiences.
Self-development is not about collecting; it is about correcting the things that you have being doing wrong.

Exercise: Make a list of all your self-development books. Write one fundamental lesson you learned from each book. Whenever you have successfully applied that lesson in your life, tick it on the list. After a month see which lesson gets the most ticks and which one doesn't get any ticks. This will reveal what you need to apply more and which books have become part of your self and which books are still just on your shelf.

Cross Roads

When we face tough decisions in life we see them as crossroads.
One way leads to the right thing and the other way leads to totally the wrong thing. We see the selections as all or nothing, and in the end no matter what we decide or choose we are rarely completely satisfied with what we have chosen… We still keep wondering what the other way would have been like.

Roundabouts

When we face choices, at times it is useful to think of them as exits on the roundabout. There are many exits, all leading to different roads.
It is about having the faith that all roads can take us to the same destination as long as we know where we want to reach. One road may be quicker, another one more scenic, another one more exciting etc. but when we know our destination it doesn't matter which road we travel on as we can eventually navigate our way and get to it.

We all face decisions in life, sometimes we get paralyzed and do nothing and stagnate.
We fear the wrong decision.

Decisions are like exits on the roundabout.
Different roads, different scenery but all can take you to your destination as long as you know where you want to get to.

Suggestion: Review a recent decision. How do you feel about it now? Are you still thinking about the other choice?

Scarcity Mentality

Scarcity mentality is thinking that there isn't enough for everyone.

When you think there isn't enough for everyone, you want to grab more for yourself so that you don't end up with less. And no matter how much you have you always feel you don't have enough, and so you don't share willingly with others and you become stingy.

Abundance Mentality

Abundance mentality is about feeling that there is plenty for everyone.

No one will miss out.

When you feel you have more than enough then you are able to share with others easily. This is not just about materialistic resources but also about your inner virtues: you easily give out love, trust, compliments to others because you feel you have enough inside of you.

When you have abundance mentality your glass remains full. When you feel abundant, you know that life will present you with enough of whatever you need.

Enough love, enough money, enough opportunities.

In life, abundance starts with your inner mental attitude before it makes its way to the outer world.

Exercise: Start the day with five minutes of abundance meditation. Focus on creating the feeling of abundance inside, saying to yourself that there is enough love, money, opportunities… for everyone… I have enough… I can give easily…

Sensibility

When someone gets upset or affected by everything they see or hear it means they are too sensitive. When someone is too sensitive all external things control their feelings and they themselves have no control over them.

Whenever someone says something slightly negative to them or criticizes them they get hugely affected by it and feel quite disturbed. They are like a leaf in a stormy sea with no control on their feelings.

Sense-Ability

Developing sense-ability means having that ability to discern what should affect our inner sense and what should not.

For example, if someone says something negative about your work and you know after reflection that their comment was not valid, then instead of getting upset or angry just let it go.

Be sense-able. Develop the ability to choose what, when and where you apply your sensitivity.

Sense-ability is the ability to sense which emotions are valid in relation to the situation and which are better to let go.

Don't be too sensitive; learn to develop sense-ability instead. Sense-ability will keep you in control of your feelings and emotions.

Try this: Next time you get upset because someone says something unpleasant to you, reflect on the comment rationally.

Impulse

Impulses rise and fade quickly. At times they are a bit like short and sharp emotional reactions to external stimulus. They usually push us to do something. It can be impulsive shopping (instant pleasure seeking) or towards angry outbursts (fighting pain).
We have all done something impulsively at one point or the other in our lives.
Most of the time, we actually don't feel that great after an impulsive indulgence.

Instinct

Instinct is deeper and longer lasting. It's something innate. It rises not with thought but with a deep gut feeling. It is not based on emotion nor on some reaction to something external. It is a deep sense of knowing that comes from within.

There are so many delicious things available to eat, so many attractive things to buy.
There are so many temptations surrounding us that if we don't know how to control our impulses we might get into a lot of trouble.

Impulse starts with an intense thought:
The more awareness we have of our thoughts the more we will be in a position to control and manage our impulses.
Instinct starts with a deep feeling:
The more we understand our own feelings the more we will be able to use our instinct.

Think about: A time when you did something impulsively and a time when you experienced a deep instinctual feeling. How can you differentiate between them in the future?

Conviction

Conviction is about our opinions. At times we are totally convinced that only our viewpoint is right. We think that we are correct and that other people are wrong.
Our convictions sometime shut down our ability to remain open-minded.

Curiosity

Curiosity allows us to explore other people's beliefs...
It is good to be curious about other ways of thinking and viewpoints. When we are curious enough to explore, then we may even find a better viewpoint.

Children are curious by nature. At birthdays and Christmas they are eager to unwrap their presents even when they don't know what is in there. They unwrap the present with great enthusiasm and excitement as if they are going to find the most wonderful thing ever ...
As children we have a lot of curiosity.
As adults we get comfortable with our old beliefs and old ways of doing things, and anything that we don't know scares us.
Remain positively curious; don't let your old convictions stop you from unwrapping the present.

I have no special talents. I am only passionately curious.
Einstein

Exercise: Think about a fixed conviction you have about something. Just for the sake of curiosity explore other people's opinions on the subject without the need to defend your conviction.

Blind Optimism

Blind optimism is when we just sit there thinking that everything will work out and do not bother with putting in any effort.
We think that thinking positively about the future is enough to achieve anything in life.
Blind optimism is dangerous; it is like driving your car blindfolded.

Optimism

Optimism means believing things are positive and good, and that what is not good now can become better with effort.
This type of thinking propels us to take positive action.
Real optimism has a good balanced view of reality and does not ignore the problems or difficulties but works towards a positive outcome.

Blind optimism is a form of self-deception which can lead to losing touch with reality.
Real optimism is about knowing the reality and remaining positive.

What we want is not blind optimism but flexible optimism – optimism with eyes open.
Martin Seligman

Suggestion: Examine your views in relation to different aspects of life. For example: Health – do you smoke, drink alcohol over the healthy limit and don't exercise… yet believe nothing detrimental will ever happen to your health – are you being blindly optimistic? Are you ignoring any another area of your life, due to blind optimism?

Tolerance

Tolerance is when we do not like someone or something but we just passively put up with it even if we feel uncomfortable or disturbed about it.

Acceptance

Acceptance is when we truly recognize someone's different way of being, or opinion or lifestyle and have the ability to appreciate it for what it is even though it might be quite different from our own.
It does not mean forcefully appreciating everything and everyone but it means allowing people or things to be as they are without causing us any personal unease.

It is better to learn to accept people and situations for what they are rather than just force yourself to tolerate them.
Tolerance can run out, acceptance remains.

Tolerance just puts up with it, secretly wanting it to be different. Acceptance allows it to be what it is and does not secretly wish for it to be any different.

Exercise: Read about different views on controversial topics.
Practise acceptance.

Careless

Careless is when we don't pay appropriate attention to things. We act irresponsibly and become uncaring.
We become clumsy, scatty, forgetful, sloppy, slack...
We do things without being observant.
When we are careless, it's like we are functioning on autopilot.
Life is too precious to be wasted carelessly.

Carefree

Carefree does not mean not caring; it means caring but without worry.
It means doing your best in the situation and then letting go of the worry attached to it.
Carefree means not wasting time on worry but at the same time being appropriately responsible and attentive towards things and people.

Being careless is a bit like avoiding responsibility but still being worried about things.
Carefree is when one takes full responsibility but wastes no time worrying.

If you want to be
bright and happy
better to be more Carefree.
If you want less mess
in life
better be less
Careless.

Life is too short for worry, be carefree.
Life may be short but it is smart enough to catch you when you have been careless.

Try this:
Once you have done everything you need to do in relation to a

project or an activity, write all your concerns on a piece of paper. Then put the paper away. Let go of all the worry about it.

Whole

When we have difficulty in one area of our life, we get so consumed by it that we make it a worry for our entire life. We stop paying attention to other important things because of it. If the problem or difficulty is at work then we need to remember we still have our home life, our relationships, our health, our social life, our spiritual life etc. to enjoy and take care of.
We should try not to spread the worry from one area of life to the whole of our life.

Slice

Everything in life is just a slice of the whole.
Everything in life only plays a part in the whole of life; it does not or perhaps it 'should not' become everything.
For example, if you don't have a romantic partner it is good to remember that there are also other areas of life: professional life, spiritual life, social life… and not having a romantic life does not mean you don't have anything else to live for.
Or if you were jobless, it would be important not to neglect your relationships, health, spiritual development while you are job hunting… and not having a job does not mean your entire life has to be on standstill.

It is good to remind ourselves that nothing is everything and everything is just a slice of the whole.

Know that however ugly the parts appear the whole remains beautiful… the wholeness of life and things, the divine beauty of the universe.
Robinson Jeffers

Exercise: Make a 'wheel of life' pie chart consisting of – Physical health, Social life, Family, Professional life, Spiritual life, Hobbies,

Self-development etc. Also add other sections that are important to you. Look at the chart as a whole. Reflect on the particular sections that you need to enhance.

Beliefs

When we accept something to be the truth, it becomes our belief.
It is our strong conviction or judgement about something.
For example: Older people cannot learn; Girls are not good at sports; All blonds are stupid etc., etc...
These are obvious and stereotypically negative... but some beliefs are not so obvious.
We all have beliefs about something or the other.
Time to time it is good to check our own internal beliefs...
and see which ones need to be discarded and which ones are worth hanging on to.

Behaviour

What we do and how we conduct ourselves is our behaviour.
We can sit there every day, all day reciting positive affirmations but unless we actually translate them into our behaviour nothing will ever change.
You can strongly believe that kindness is a virtue, but if you shout unkindly at the first person that annoys you then your beliefs don't match your behaviour.

You can collect an amazing set of beliefs, and strongly believe in things such as:
'Being rich and making money is easy'; 'One should follow their dreams'; 'Regular exercise is good for you'...
These are great beliefs but are you – making money? Following your dreams? Exercising regularly?
Beliefs are just internal opinions; behaviour is about actual practice.

Your beliefs don't make you a better person; your behaviour does...
Anonymous

Exercise: Examine your beliefs. Which ones are negative beliefs that need discarding and which ones are positive beliefs lacking practice?

Love (noun)

We all want love and we are all on some kind of perpetual quest to 'find' love.
We think that love is perhaps a person, place or a thing.
We keep looking for that person, that place or acquiring that thing that will give us love... we keep searching for that feeling.

Love (verb)

Love is about doing and a way of being.
It does not come from a person, place or a thing. It comes from doing and being.
'Do love' and 'be love' is different from 'want love'.

Love is not a noun but a verb.
Love cannot be named, acquired, possessed, bought, visited.
It can only ever be given, received and lived.

Love is a verb. Love is something you do; the sacrifices you make, the giving of self.
If you want to study love, study those who sacrifice for others.
Love – the feeling – is a fruit of love the verb...
Stephen Covey

Think about: Who and what do you love? Is it a noun, is it a verb, is it a bird, is it a plane?

Waiting

We are all waiting for something to happen. Waiting means just passively wishing for things to turn out OK. It is just wishful thinking and nothing more.
Waiting is useless.

Patience

Patience means the ability to have a good proactive attitude while you are waiting.
Patience means persevering with all your efforts even when nothing is happening. It means remaining positive when everything looks bleak and continuing with the hard work knowing that one day it will happen.

Patience means remaining positive and undisturbed and carrying on doing and not giving up even when there are no signs of progress. Patience comes from internal trust that things will be fine.
Waiting is just sitting around doing nothing and thinking: the timing is not right, I can't do anything now, the circumstances are not right now...
Patience is a virtue; waiting is useless and a waste of time.

Patience is waiting, not passively waiting. That is laziness. But to keep going when the going is hard and slow – that is patience.
Leo Tolstoy

Try this: Next time something gets delayed. Examine – are you just waiting or being patient?

Intuition

Intuition is that gut feeling that tells us what is right without the need for conscious reasoning.
Intuition is like a sixth sense. We only feel and sense it sometimes.
It would be amazing to have an inner sixth sense navigating us through our life all the time!
Intuition is important but the problem is that it is not that easy to access.

In Tuition

It is perhaps useful to think of intuition as being in tuition or guidance from the inner self.
In order to be guided by the inner self, we have to listen to it.
In order to listen to the inner self, we have to stop the noise on the outside.
In order to stop the noise on the outside, we have to be in silence.
In order to be in silence, we have to learn to still the mind.
In order to still the mind, we have to meditate...

Intuition is the deep knowing within us that has all the answers already.
We just have to learn how to access it.

Meditation connects us to our intuition.
It is like being in tuition with our inner self.

Exercise: Practise meditation and try to feel the deep inner guidance. Pay attention to what it is saying and connect with it.

Happiness-fix

Happiness-fix is about hedonic gratification. It is about constantly seeking pleasure that comes from buying something new, approval from others, alcohol, drugs, food… it is about instant gratification. This gratification is short-lived – it does not last long. Therefore dependency on this type of gratification means constantly chasing happiness from external things – people, objects or activities.

In order to have that momentary 'happiness-fix' to stay on the hedonic treadmill we keep buying new things, we constantly crave attention from others and keep seeking new experiences to give us that momentary 'happiness fix'.

Happiness-fixed

Happiness-fixed is eudemonic well-being.

We feel a deeper level of contentment and satisfaction with life when we pursue meaning, self-development and self-actualization.

Eudemonic well-being comes from following a meaningful life rather than chasing a pleasurable life.

Pleasure is not the only criteria for a satisfied life. Growth that comes from facing challenges, experiencing pain and sadness also contributes to a higher level of connection with one's own meaning of life.

Happiness-fixed is fixed.

Sadness and grief do not reduce it and pleasure does not enhance it. All experiences contribute to it equally.

Happiness-fix is about constantly chasing things that yield pleasure – commodities, people, situations…
Happiness-fixed is about personal growth, self-acceptance, meaning and purpose…

Just as the good life is something beyond the pleasant life, the meaningful life is beyond the good life.
Martin Seligman

Exercise: Write down five things that give purpose and meaning to your life. Also write down five different things that give you pleasure. Reflect on the differences.

Of this World

Being 'of this world' means making materialistic fulfilment life's ultimate pursuit. Allowing greed, lust, rivalry, indulgence, jealously, competition, envy, glut... to be part of everyday life.

It means to be driven solely by external materialistic desires and living without any conscious awareness of inner responsibility.

In this World

Being 'in this world' not only means being fully present, it means to participate in what is happening around us with full conscious responsibility. Being consciously responsive means to carry out everyday stuff that is needed to function in this world, with responsibility and best intention.

It means to respond to situations with positivity and not allowing attachment to materialistic things to negatively influence our actions or thoughts.

Being 'of this world' means getting lost in the minutia of existence. Being 'in this world' means to live a consciously aware life so that the external pleasures and worries do not affect our inner being.

Better to live in the world, but not be filled by it.
A ship lives in the water; but if the water gets into the ship, she goes to the bottom.
Dwight L. Moody

Exercise: During the day stop every two to three hours and draw your attention to the present moment. Become consciously aware of your thoughts and what is happening around you. Go within and fully charge your inner positivity and then go out 'in this world' again.

Beautiful

Something that is nice to see or aesthetically pleasing is considered beautiful.

A lot of people are preoccupied with the desire to look beautiful. They think for a person or especially for a woman to be beautiful she must be good looking on the outside and have a perfectly proportionate body.

Beauty-full

Being beauty-full means being full of beauty on the inside.

Being 'beautiful' on the outside is just about appearance.

Appearance is just aesthetics.

Aesthetics is just about measurements and proportions.

True beauty is a lot more than just measurements.

True beauty is what beauty does.

Beauty is not about millimetres, centimetres, pounds or kilos.
It is about modesty, confidence, pleasantness and kindness.

The beauty of a woman is not in a facial mode
but the true beauty in a woman is reflected in her soul.
It is the caring that she lovingly gives, the passion that she shows.
The beauty of a woman grows with the passing years.
Audrey Hepburn

Exercise:

1) Notice positive gestures of other people towards you. Appreciate the inner beauty of their gesture.

2) Notice the natural beauty in faces around you. Kind eyes, generous smile, carefree laughter, cute talk...

Preacher

Preaching is about reciting a lot of positive quotes in conversation, posting loads of positive sayings and motivational videos on social media but not actually applying anything in real life.

Some people preach a lot of nice things but do not follow any of it themselves.

If you say nice stuff, read nice books and post nice things on your social media but don't apply any of it in your actual life then you are just a phony preacher.

Practitioner

These days people think posting loads of nice quotes and sayings on social media makes one a true positivity practitioner.

It's no good trying to influence how others behave if you don't apply anything you say to your own life.

A good practitioner practises what they preach.

Practising is doing what you say and saying what you do.

Leading by example is the best practice.
People usually follow examples not advice.
Practise is more effective than preaching.

You enter the path of transformation when you begin to practise the things you pronounce.
Thich Nhat Hanh

Try this: Find three quotes or sayings you like. Check if you are practising them yourself. Which one could you put more into practice?

Listening for Self

Listening for self is when we listen to gather information that may be useful for us. This type of listening is helpful when we are learning something new or attending a lecture.
Listening for self in a conversation means listening just to construct a reply.
Listening for self is about our own needs.

Listening for Others

Listening for others means to listen to understand the deeper meaning of what someone is saying and what they want to express. It is not just about their words. It includes their body language, their tone, their expression, their breathing... their sentiment. It also includes what they don't say.
Listening for others is about the needs of the other person.
Sometimes we just need to listen for others.

Think about what type of listening you need to do in a specific situation...
Listening for self or listening for others?

Listening for self is about what will benefit you from the conversation.
Listening for others is about fully understanding what the other person needs to express.

Exercise: Before launching into your next long conversation try to become aware of what type of listening you need to do and when.

Nobody

Everybody wants to be somebody.
No one wants to be nobody.
Nobody is just anybody.
Treat everybody as somebody.

Somebody

Everybody is somebody.
If you want to be somebody don't treat yourself just like anybody.
You are not just anybody, you are somebody.

We are all unique and we all have something that others don't. Even two branches of the same tree are not identical, let alone any two human beings.
There will only ever be one you in this entire universe.

One of the greatest diseases is to be nobody to somebody.
Mother Teresa

Do: Go out today and talk to anybody who you don't know. Find out things about them so that they turn into somebody that you will know.

Closed Hearted

Some experiences can lead us to close our heart.
Closed-hearted means to live with suspicion, animosity, mistrust, caution, hate and avoidance...
It means to be closed off towards new experiences and people because of fear and doubt.

Open Hearted

Being open-hearted is living with positivity, clarity and love.
It means embracing new experiences and new people with confidence and trust.
It means not allowing the bad events of the past to constrain the quality of what you need to experience in the present and in the future.

Living with a closed heart is a bit like never getting out of your car.
It's like driving through the most beautiful scenery but never stepping out to smell or feel the places.

You open your heart knowing that there's a chance it may be broken one day and in opening your heart, you experience a love and joy that you never dreamed possible.
Bob Marley

Idea: Attend a gallery or an exhibition on your own, talk to someone new or a stranger. With an open heart, listen to their opinion and thoughts about the displays or artwork. Engage with them openly; try not to form judgements.

Weakness

Weakness is the inner guardedness that results from fear of pain and hurt.
When someone is weak they are scared to share their authentic self and only present a small part of who they are to the world.
They fear rejection and disapproval, and therefore do not have the courage to be their true self.

Vulnerability

Vulnerability is our inner emotional susceptibility towards pain and hurt.
Being vulnerable means to have the courage to be who you are despite the chance of pain, hurt, disapproval or rejection.
Vulnerability is a strength because it allows us to be authentic and our true self.

Vulnerability is natural as we are all vulnerable in some way.
Weakness is not natural as we are all born with tremendous potential.
Embracing vulnerability means not allowing weakness to stop us from living fully.

When we embrace our own vulnerability we allow ourselves to be free.

Suggestion: Identify a situation or activity in which you generally don't participate due to shyness or fear. Visualize yourself taking part and allow yourself to feel vulnerable… What's the worst that can happen?

Trigger Switch

Some people seem to have the switch to trigger your inner annoyance. It's like as soon as they press a button, your inner annoyance is triggered… you become irritated and perhaps even angry at them.

If this happens a lot it means that lots of people out there are walking around with your inner trigger switch and you yourself don't have any control over it.

Blessing Button

When someone or something irritates you, just remember to take away the trigger switch from them and press your own blessing button. Blessing button is your own secret switch that changes the irritation into a blessing. Only you have control over it.

You just need to ask yourself, 'What is it about this person or situation that I find so irritating? What does it reveal to me about me?'

The answer is your blessing.

When we get annoyed and irritated with someone it is usually about our own stuff rather than the other person.

If you are irritated by every rub, how will you be polished?
Rumi

Try this: Next time you get irritated press your blessing button.

Talk More

We all love to talk and give our opinions in conversations. We feel that just by talking more we are adding more value to the conversation. Sometimes we get so occupied with giving our own opinion that we don't really hear what others are saying.

Contribute More

Contributing more to a conversation does not necessarily mean talking or saying more. It actually means listening more attentively. Supporting and encouraging others by nodding or smiling. Contributing more is less about your own opinions and more about responding to what others say in a mindful way.

Talking more does not always mean that you are contributing more.

At times in order to add real value to a conversation we have to listen more, support more, encourage more and smile more.

Think less, talk less, but contribute more.

Try this: Next time you have the opportunity to be a part of a group conversation, try to say less but contribute more.

I want Peace

Everyone wants to feel peaceful. We all seek peace. We think we will experience peace when external things in our lives are sorted. We think the feeling of peace comes from outside when everything is calm and there are no dramas happening.

I am Peace

Peace is not something out there, it is in you. You yourself are Peace!
When you become peaceful, you will experience peace.
Say to yourself, 'I AM a being of peace. I feel peace all around me and within me.'
Say it a few times with true belief.

I AM is a powerful statement.
It is more powerful than I wish, I want, I desire, I deserve…

Don't seek peace. Be peace.
I am Peace.

Do: Sit in silence for few minutes. Try to turn down the chatter in the mind and for a few minutes, just be… just be… just be peace.

Grudge

Holding on to unkind words means you yourself are doing more harm to yourself than the person who actually said those words to you. Perhaps they only said the unkind words once to you but you keep repeating them in your head again and again...
You are more unkind to yourself than the other person.

Gratitude

Gratitude is inclusive. It includes all experiences good and bad. To practise gratitude means to be thankful not only for the good things but also for the unkind words that someone said to you. Perhaps those unkind words have taught you something or shown you another path... perhaps those unkind words have made you realize something or made you see something from a different perspective... When you apply true gratitude you are not only kind to others but also to yourself.

Don't hold on to grudges, convert them into gratitude.
A grateful person sees all adversity as a useful lesson.

Reflect upon your present blessings, of which every man has plenty;
not on your past misfortunes, of which all men have some.
Charles Dickens

Suggestion: Examine what grudges you are holding on to. Write them down on a sheet of paper in a column. In the next column write down one positive thing, no matter how small, that came about due to the negative experience related to that grudge or that person.

Play

Be Interesting

Sometimes we think good conversation is about impressing someone. So when we talk to someone for the first time we want to appear interesting.
We want to impress the other person with our stories. We want them to think we lead an interesting life so we start telling them about our job, amazing adventures, exotic holidays, our unique hobbies etc.
We forget to ask about their life, and even when they are telling us something about their life we are internally just thinking about what to tell them next.

Be Interested

Good conversation is about good listening and being genuinely interested in what the other person has to say. It is about wanting to know about them and having a healthy curiosity.
Being interested in what someone has to say involves good listening and asking the right questions.
In a conversation it is far more important to be interested in what the person is saying than trying to make yourself look interesting.

We get so preoccupied by wanting to appear interesting to other people that we forget to be interested in them or what they are saying.
There is a difference between talking 'at' someone and talking 'with' someone.

The trick to impress people is to be interested in them! People usually get more easily impressed when someone shows real interest in them rather than when someone tries to impress them with their own stories.

Exercise: In a social conversation become aware of the balance between appearing interesting and being interested. Notice your own communications as well as others'.

Until then...

Until then is about the destination.
Destination is something in the future. How much in the future, we don't know. Could be tomorrow, next month, next year... in 5 years' time, 10 years... or never.
Are you putting off something 'until' you reach the destination:
Until I buy a house...
Until I get married...
Until I have X amount of money...
'Until then' is a road leading to never ever land.

Be now!

Be now is about the Journey.
The Journey of your life is precious.
You don't know how long or short is your journey. It could be 100 years, the next 40 years, 5 years, 2 months, 1 week or just until tomorrow...
Whatever is happening 'now' is your life.
Appreciate whatever you see now...
Love whatever you are doing now...
Be happy now...
Be now...

'Happiness is a journey and not the destination'.
Such a cliché! Yet sadly so many of us don't get it at all!
We keep waiting for perfect circumstances...

Journey of life is only one way and we can't ever return to the moments that have already passed.
Embrace whatever there is in your life right now.
No matter whatever the circumstances are.
'Now' is both the journey and the destination.

Exercise: List all your 'until then' statements. Identify what you are putting off and why.

Cold

A cold person does not express their true feelings.
They try to portray a cool persona by hiding or suppressing what's underneath.
They are usually referred to as being self-absorbed, aloof, unfeeling, uncaring, closed, critical, unapproachable etc.
It's not considered cool to be cold!

Cool

Being 'cool' is good.
A cool person is usually liked by all.
Everyone wants to be cool…
In reality being cool is actually about being 'warm'!
A cool person is caring, confident, friendly, genuine and charming.

People who are cold need the most warmth.
People who are cool have the warmest heart.

The difference between being a 'cool' and 'cold' person is that of inner warmth.
If you want to be a cool person, create inner warmth.

Think about: Someone you know personally who is really cool.
What inner qualities make him/her cool?

Mistakes

Mistakes are a part of life. Everyone has made a misjudgement, miscalculation or misinterpretation at one time or another in his or her life.
Mistakes can cause a lot of grief.
Guilt, shame, blame can stop a person from trying again. When someone does not try again, a mistake forever remains a mistake.

Missed Takes

If we view mistakes as 'missed takes', then the next time the same chance appears we can just retake it again.
This provides the opportunity to do the thing correctly.
Misjudgement is just missed judgement.
Miscalculation is just missed calculation.
Misinterpretation is just missed interpretation.

Treat a mistake like a missed take. Don't lose time in blaming, shaming, naming.
Allow yourself or the other person the chance to retake the missed take again so that error can be corrected.

If you don't make any mistakes you won't learn anything new and when you don't learn anything new you will keep repeating the same mistakes over and over again.

Think about: A mistake you made and a lesson you learned from it, and how you applied the lesson later.

Distraction

When we are stressed we engage in certain activities thinking that these activities will remove our stress. Watching movies, going for a holiday, shopping, drinking alcohol and going to restaurants... There is nothing at all wrong with these activities; but they don't actually remove stress, they are just momentary distractions. When the activity finishes we return back to the same level of stress as before. We are just temporarily lulled into a false sense of calm by these external distractions.

Relaxation

Relaxation that removes mental stress is achieved by relaxing the mind. Relaxation of the mind comes from withdrawing from activity and slowing the thought process. It is achieved by reducing engagement and enhancing inner stillness. Regular relaxation for the mind is very important for our inner stability.

Going shopping, watching a movie, dining in a restaurant, going to an exhibition... these may be positive distractions but these are not relaxation strategies.
We need to create time for real relaxation and not just distractions.
Real mental relaxation needs inner and outer silence.

We need to learn how to relax, especially when there seems to be no time or place for it.
A few moments of inner relaxation can be practised anywhere and at any time.

Try this: Incorporate regular 'mini refreshers' in your daily routine. Stop every four hours from whatever you are doing for just five minutes. Sit silently and breathe deeply. Put all stresses aside for five minutes without using any distractions.

IT Abuse

Over the past decade technology has had a major impact on our everyday life. We are using Facebook, Twitter, WhatsApp, Snapchat, Skype etc. more and more to relate to others. This is also having an impact on how we relate to our own selves.
Some people are constantly engaged in posting, updating, commenting on social media because their sense of self is derived from what is happening online. They get negatively affected by comparing their own life with what they see as the life of others on the media. Some people don't realize that their way of using IT is causing harm to themselves.

IT Use

New technology is a fantastic. tool
However, it is important to remember that IT is just a 'tool' and not a 'way of being'.
When used correctly, a tool can enhance life in many wonderful ways.
We now have so many ways to say 'I care' to someone. We can post that on Facebook, tweet it, Snapchat it, WhatsApp it etc., etc… We can be so creative with our communications. It is great to use technology to enhance communication in new ways.

We need to use IT mindfully and positively.
Not only in respect of others but for our own self as well.
It is important to use IT consciously, rather than unconsciously allow yourself to be abused by it.

Facebook, Twitter, WhatsApp etc. – so many more ways to say and mean more to each other.
Are you saying and meaning more to each other?

Think about: How you communicate with the world using social media. Are you using it well or are you being used by it?

Roller Coaster Ride

Roller coaster ride is fun. We go up and we go down. We scream and we shout. We laugh and we cry. It is all exciting and thrilling.

A roller coaster is just for amusement, it doesn't actually take us anywhere. The ups and downs of a roller coaster are for entertainment. They don't make us a better rider.

Road Journey

A road also has twists and turns, hills and slopes... the sceneries also change but the main thing is that the road eventually leads to somewhere. On the road we need to learn to drive our vehicle and adjust to the twists and turns and the ups and downs. All these eventually make us a better driver.

A roller coaster life can appear thrilling but it will not get you to your destination.
Going up and down too many times will eventually make you sick.

Sometimes we get addicted to a roller coaster life.
We crave lots of drama, variety of thrills and constant excitement...
When you want to go from A to Z, don't get stuck on a roller coaster ride.
Roller coasters are fun, but they won't take you anywhere.

Exercise: Write down what you would like to achieve over the next three years. Draw a hypothetical map of the three-year road journey. Mark the foreseeable ups and downs. Write down all the skills and resources you will need for your road journey.

Everything

There are so many possibilities around us. So many things look interesting and engaging that we want to do everything.
We want to buy everything, we want to see everything, we want to know everything.
We want to be involved in everything and we want to experience everything...
Everything is not possible.

Anything

Success comes from believing you can do anything.
Being able to do anything does not mean you have to do everything.
It means you have the ability to do whatever it takes to get to your goals.

Doing anything is a matter of motivation.
Doing everything is matter of provocation.

Believing one can do anything is about a mindset. Knowing one must not end up doing everything is about mindfulness.

Think about: If you could do anything tomorrow (for the entire day) what would you be doing? What would you not be doing?

Daily Action

Daily actions are duties, tasks that we have to repeat again and again day after day.
Sometimes all that we do in our daily life just ends up as part of a day-to-day timetable.
Everyday actions become a regular routine. Routines often become mundane, boring, dull, tedious, and repetitive...

Daily Adventure

Adventure is about exploration and discovery.
We don't necessarily have to be on an exotic holiday or location to experience adventure.
Daily activity can be turned into daily adventure by discovering new ways to do the same thing.
Life is exciting with daily adventure... It brings newness and freshness.

Daily adventure is not about seeking novelty for the sake of it but about bringing newness and freshness.
It is about experiencing the same thing differently and finding new perspectives.

The real voyage of discovery consists not in seeking new landscapes, but in having new eyes.
Marcel Proust

Idea: Examine something that you do every day in the same way. Change it in some way and do it differently for next few days.

Having More

Having more means more clutter. The more things you have the more things you have to worry about and take care of. Then you end up having less time to do the things you want to do.

The more things you have the less you actually use them.

If you have 100 pairs of shoes, in order to use them all equally in a year, you would wear one pair for three days only. Imagine how many years a pair of shoes will last if you only wore it for three days each year...

Doing More

The less clutter you have to take care of in life, the more time you actually have to do the things you want to do.

Less stuff also means more usage.

If you have 10 pairs of shoes you would wear each pair for 36 days a year in order to use them all equally.

Doing more begins with having less.
Have less and use more.

If you own loads of stuff then remember those things will eventually end up owning you and your time.

Do: Decide a date for a decluttering day. Note it in your diary. On the day go through your wardrobe and cupboards and pull out all the stuff that you don't use and no longer need. Reduce your clutter. Own less, do more.

Long Vacations

Long vacation means being off work for several days or weeks at a stretch. For some people this is such a rare occurrence that they binge on their travel during these days.
Their travel becomes purely about the distance covered, air miles gained, number of cities seen, countries visited...
Long vacations often mean living your desired life before one gets back to the 'reality' of their daily job.

Mini Retirements

Mini retirement is about fully stopping for a period of time. It means to stop and reassess everything in your life.
It is not just about travel or relaxation. It can be about learning something new or studying again for a period of time or just 'being'.
It's about doing the things that you think you will only have the time to do when you retire.
Why wait until the end of your career to do what you really want to do?
Take mini retirements and do some of the stuff you have always wanted to do.

Long vacation just means cramming in loads of experience into a few days before getting back to the reality of the daily job.
Mini retirement is different. It is not just about doing some stuff while you are off work.
It is about completely stopping the routine for a period of time and doing the things that you dream of doing when you retire.

Don't leave things that you have always wanted to do for later... Who knows if we will ever get there. Do them now.

Exercise: Make a list of things you would like to do when you retire. It doesn't matter how young or old you are. Just think about things you like to do if/when you no longer have to go to work. How could you do some of them now?

Confrontation

Confrontation happens when two parties have some type of a disagreement or dispute. They clash in their opinion or some idea. Both parties want to be right and prove the other wrong, and this can lead to a fight.
Confrontation does not feel nice as it often involves anger or aggression.

Challenge

A challenge in a game is about getting involved and playing the game, and not about fighting in order to win.
When there is a confrontation in a relationship it is better to imagine it being like a challenge in a game.
Your motive is not about winning by fighting. Your challenge is to say things in such a way that it does not upset the other person. Your challenge is also about keeping the relationship intact and not damaging it by saying things that you may regret later.

In a healthy relationship, partners may challenge each other at times.
Challenge is good, it's an opportunity for mutual growth.
In an unhealthy relationship partners keep confronting each other.
Confrontation is not good; it's about proving the other wrong and winning.

Challenges are good for relationships, confrontations are not. Challenge each other but don't confront.

Try this: Next time you feel you are starting to disagree with someone, immediately shift the focus from confrontation to challenge. It's your challenge to say things in such a way that it does not upset the other person.

Reading Another's Mind

Sometimes do you find yourself doing a bit of mind reading?
He is thinking that I am silly.
She thinks my work is not good enough.
They hate my presentation.
Well how do you know all this?
Can you read someone's mind?

Minding My Own Business

When you find yourself doing mind reading... just tell yourself to mind your own business. You wouldn't want others to read your thoughts so don't try to read theirs...
When you start thinking things like...
He is thinking that I am silly.
She thinks my work is not good enough.
They hate my presentation.
... Just say to yourself: 'Let me mind my own business.'

When we start assuming all the negative stuff others are thinking about us, let's remember we cannot go inside someone's mind and read their thoughts.
So let's not start assuming what others are thinking.

Never assume, because when you assume, you make an ASS of U and ME.
Jerry Belson

Exercise: Observe yourself during the day. How many times are you 'mind reading'? When you are mind reading what kind of stuff you are assuming?

Enjoy

Enjoying yourself is about pleasure. Pleasure and fun are good, but life is not always full of fun activities.
When we chase fun and pleasure all the time we can get disappointed very quickly. We think everything should be fun and exciting. This is not realistic. Some things in life are not about fun.
When we don't feel fun and pleasure in doing something, we easily get bored. Feeling bored is not great; it is the opposite of enjoy.

In-Joy

Being in-joy is about being happy with whatever there is. Being in-joy means doing everything with joy regardless of what the task is. It is not about chasing fun and pleasurable activities all the time; it is about creating inner joy so even when you are involved with something that is not particularly fun or exciting you can still be in-joy whilst doing it.
Inner joy is about you, not the activity.

Focus on creating inner joy in your life. Enjoyment will follow.

Enjoyment is about the activity, being in-joy is about you. When you are in-joy, you can enjoy everything.

Suggestion: Think about an activity you don't enjoy. How could you do it in a way that you would find joy whilst doing it? Example: Listening to your favourite type of music whilst cleaning…

Boldness

Boldness often means having no fear.
We all have some fear about something or the other.
To eradicate absolutely all fear before we do something new is not always possible.
Sometimes being reckless or rebellious is misinterpreted as boldness.

Courage

Courage does not mean having no fear.
Courage is about feeling the fear but being passionate enough to do whatever needs to be done.

Boldness is impatient. It is about doing what it takes as long as the desired result is in sight.
Courage is patient. It is about doing what it takes even when the desired result may not be certain.

I learned that courage was not the absence of fear, but the triumph over it.
The brave man is not he who does not feel afraid, but he who conquers that fear.
Nelson Mandela

Think about: Someone who you think is courageous. What other qualities do they have?

Coconut

Coconut is hard on the outside, and soft and hollow inside.

Peach

Peach is soft on the outside but its core is strong and solid.

Often we hear that to be a softie inside is a quality.
A softie gets affected by everything that is on the outside.
Being hard inside does not mean being cold and rigid. It means to be solid and stable inside.
Being soft outside means to be gentle and empathetic with everyone.

Far better to be a Peach.
You might get crushed and bruised on the outside but you remain solid and intact inside.
A Coconut once cracked loses all its inner fluid.

Think about: Are you a coconut or a peach?

Examination

When we meet someone new, or we start a new job or we are in any other new situation… we start an internal examination.
We start scrutinizing.
We start dissecting what's good or bad, what we like or dislike about the situation or the person. We start an internal process in our head to arrive at a conclusion of whether we finally like or dislike the person or the situation.
It's like an internal examination and the person or the situation has to either pass or fail.

Exploration

Exploration is about finding the different qualities of the person or the situation.
When we explore something there is no pass or fail. It is not about having a conclusive opinion about the person or the situation, it's just finding out different things about them.

Explore all situations and people with eagerness, don't just examine them.
Constant examination can lead to exhaustion.
Be an explorer not an examiner.

Exploration is not just about trotting off to the opposite side of the world discovering some indigenous tribes.
Exploration starts with your next-door neighbour.

Suggestion: Connect with someone who is from a different culture or has different interests. Explore their culture or interests. Don't think about liking or disliking things, just explore.

Controlling Time

Controlling time is about time management.

It is about managing time so that we can do all the things we have to do.

When you want to control time you list all the things that need to be done then set a timetable for everything.

Creating Time

Creating time is about time availability.

It is about freeing time so you can do the things you want to do.

You create time by listing all the things that are not important in your life.

You then cross out the unnecessary stuff and stop doing it.

Creating time is not about saving or pinching scraps of time from here and there.

It is about letting go of all the unnecessary things that suck your precious life away.

You create time when you have a 'not to do list', when you cross out all the unimportant and useless stuff from your life.

Exercise: Write down a 'not to do list' and create some time in your life.

E.g. Stop watching useless YouTube videos. Read news daily – not hourly – thinking about what others think...

Risk

In life the probability of something bad happening at any time is perpetual.
Risk means exposure to danger or to something bad. The reality is that anything bad could happen at any time.
Known risks such as smoking, drugs, alcohol, speeding, gambling etc. are different from assumed risks. Assumed risks are make-believe risks, like imagining negative things all the time. Such as being hit by a car if you ride a bike, catching a disease if you travel to a different country, losing your job if you ask for a pay rise...

Chance

In life the probability of something amazing happening at any time is also perpetual.
Chance is about the possibility of an opportunity appearing randomly.
Anything amazing could happen at any time.
You might meet someone famous today. You might win something this week. You might find or discover something valuable this month.
Possibilities exist everywhere and every day of our lives.

Some level of risk exists with almost everything in life. Rather than focusing just on risks, think about all the wonderful chances and possibilities that also exist in everyday life.

When you want to achieve something in life, don't start thinking about all the risks.
Just allow yourself the chance to do it.

Try this: Next time you are hesitating in doing something say to yourself, 'There is a risk that this might fail, they may not like me, it might be painful... but I will allow myself at least a chance that it might turn out alright...'

Substance Abuse

Substance abuse is when we misuse stuff in a way that can be harmful for us.
Usually this refers to alcohol and drug addiction.
In everyday life we misuse a lot more than just alcohol and drugs.
The list can be extensive – Internet, social media, TV, food, shopping etc.
Example: Online shopping is great, it is effortless but a lot of people are overdoing it. It's causing them financial worries and losses.

Substance Use

Substance use means using the stuff in a sensible way and getting the best out of it.
Time to time it is a good idea to review how we use our stuff.
Online shopping, social media, surfing the net, watching TV, food, adventure, sports… etc.

Substance abuse does not just relate to drugs and alcohol.
It can also be related to other everyday activities.

Substance abuse is about escaping reality, it is not just about alcohol or drugs.
We can misuse a lot of other things in our life in order to escape reality:
Addiction to social media, online shopping, TV, food, Internet…

Think about: How you use social media, online shopping, TV, food, Internet etc. in your life.

Monotony

In life there are periods when nothing exciting seems to be happening. There are no parties to go to, no holidays booked, no functions or events coming up… nothing different, everything just same-same. When we are not constantly engaged with some type of activity we get bored easily. Boredom breeds monotony.

Non-activity

We consider non-activity to be boring. Life does not have to be filled with constant dramas, emergencies, events, celebrations, parties, festivals, birthdays.
It is good to stop time to time and be still for a while.
In periods when nothing much is happening, instead of getting restless it is better to savour the stillness and the joy of non-activity.

Life is not just about events, occasions, celebrations, parties, problems, emergencies.
The quiet periods of non-activity are equally important.

Monotony does not come from lack of excitement.
It comes from lack of appreciation of the stillness of non-activity.

Suggestion: Next time you have a quiet period for few days don't rush to fill the time with social activity for the sake of it. Just be still for a while and be with yourself, go for quiet walks, read, meditate… Use the quiet period to refresh and revive from within.

Experience

Everything we have received from the world around us is experience.
Whatever we have seen, observed, felt, gained, learned, encountered, undergone, perceived, understood… all are experiences.
We receive experience from the world around us.

Creativity

Whatever we give out into the world is our creativity.
Whatever we do, say, how we respond, express, act, produce, build, teach, innovate, make… is all our creativity. We are the creators all our thoughts, actions, our conversations, our responses.
Our creativity goes from inside of us to the world around us.

Whatever experience we receive good or bad, it is up to us to create something amazing with it.
We create our own thoughts every single second, and we also create our responses to the world around us.
Be creative, create something positive, something good.

Experience is the raw material that you receive from the world outside.
Creativity is what you do with that raw material.

Think about: Your life, how could you be more creative? With your words, actions, responses…

Joker

Joker is someone who likes telling jokes all the time. Their joking is not so much about making other people happy but is more about proving their own cleverness to others. A joker does not care about the actual situation. Their aim is to prove to others how funny he/she can be in any situation. Playfulness is good but being a clown all the time is not cool. It can become tiring for others.

Jolly

Jolly means being cheerful and happy, remaining positive and bright.
A jolly person is light-hearted and good-humoured.
Being light-hearted does not mean ignoring the seriousness of the situation.
It means applying the right level of levity or humour as appropriate to the situation.
A jolly person sees brightness in everything but they don't make fun of everything.

It is nice to hear a joke or two, but no one wants to laugh endlessly all the time.

Don't try to become a joker. Remain jolly instead.

Suggestion: Cheer up a friend who is going through a difficult time by injecting some humour and jokes. Carefully balance between taking things too seriously and not giving them appropriate importance.

Mr Right

Are you waiting for Mr Right?
Who is Mr Right?
Is Mr or Miss Right someone who takes care of you, someone who encourages you, loves you unconditionally, who wants the best for you, who allows you to grow, who gives you security… keeps you safe, is always by your side…
Do all those things come from someone else on the outside?

Me Right

Are you 'Right' yourself?
Are you someone… who can take care of someone, encourage someone with whatever they want to do regardless of what you think, are you capable of giving unconditional love… are you secure and stable within yourself completely?
Do you love yourself enough not to allow any negative thinking, can you accept another person in your life just as they are without wanting to change anything about them in any way?

It is not just about finding the right person.
It is also about becoming the right person yourself.
Are you capable and ready for giving unconditional love to yourself and to the other?

Don't worry if you haven't found Mr Right/Miss Right, there is nothing wrong with you.
However, in the meantime just focus on becoming Mr Right/Miss Right yourself first.

Think about: What qualities and strengths are you looking for in a partner? Which ones do you have yourself?

Connection

These days we can be directly connected to over thousands of people on various online platforms. Most of these people we do not meet in real life but we can communicate with them on a daily basis.

An online connection can be made instantly.

Friend

A friend is someone who you can call at odd hours of the day or night for no particular reason…

It can take a lifetime to develop a true friendship and to call someone a true friend.

It is good to have a variety of connections in your network.
Some you have met briefly, some you haven't met yet.
Some are acquaintances of someone else you know….
Some are just people you would like to know…
Some are your past classmates, some can be your future colleagues…
Amidst all this variety of connections, it is important not to lose sight of that one true friend.

You can have thousands of connections online instantly, but it is a privilege of a lifetime to become and call someone a true friend.

Do: Switch off from online social media today for a while and call a true friend that you haven't spoken to for some time.

Decluttering

Decluttering relates to material objects. It is about getting rid of all those things that are of no use to you anymore. It is about creating physical space in your environment.

It is good to declutter or spring clean time-to-time.

It is also good to observe how quickly the clutter actually seeps back in and how much new stuff you end up collecting again…

Minimalizing

Minimalizing isn't just about external stuff. It is about internal attitude. It isn't about somehow making do with less, or getting rid of excess. It is about wanting less in the first place.

It is about reducing the need or desire to collect and possess excessive physical stuff.

It means reducing attachment to things and objects, and reducing consumption.

Decluttering is about knowing what to get rid of.
Minimalizing is about knowing what not to collect in the first place.

The less you need, the lighter you will feel.
The lighter you feel the less you will need.

Exercise: Identify three items that you have not used for a while.
Ask yourself three questions:
If I went shopping would I buy this again?
Does it serve a purpose now?
Will I use it ever?
Then decide what you will do – keep it/get rid of it?

Expensive

When we say that something is expensive, it is related to the amount of money you pay for acquiring it.
Something might be very expensive but not very valuable...

Valuable

Value of something is not about money; it is about the importance of it in your life.
Don't just go after expensive things, think about their value.
How relevant are they to your life?
How valuable will the new expensive sunglasses be in your life, next to the other five you already have?

A diamond is more expensive than a bottle of water.
We don't need diamonds to survive.

A relationship is not fostered by buying expensive gifts.
It is nurtured by offering small regular gestures of value.

Do: Buy something small, an inexpensive item for a friend, that you think will have great value for them. Give it to them with a handwritten note.

Fireworks

Now and then, we all fantasize about doing something super amazing, something big, something outstanding!
We want glittering fame, super stardom, big fortune... We want to be on the cover of magazines, in TV shows, in the news...
We all want spectacular fireworks!

Sparks

Now and then, we all get tiny sparks of inspiration and ideas but we don't give them enough attention. They just fade away and we let them die.
Sparks fade as they are fleeting in nature, but their job is to light a bigger fire.
Nurture those initial sparks, don't let them die. Allow the tiny sparks of your initial ideas to light your Olympic flame!

There is no firework without the work.
If you want amazing explosions first learn to ignite your inner sparks.

Tiny sparks can together light up the entire sky with a spectacular firework.
A spectacular firework is just a bunch of sparks.

Do: Write down five recent ideas you have had. Then arrange them in order. Which one is the most achievable? Then write down three simple actions in relation to it.

Nowhere

Mind goes here, there, everywhere and nowhere, but Mind most likes to visit Nowhere.
Nowhere is where all random, negative and wasteful thoughts live.
When the Mind visits Nowhere often, it gets to know all the random, negative and wasteful thoughts very well.
Nowhere has lots of past scenarios and future fantasies.
Nowhere is an expensive place to visit, it costs a lot of time and energy.
Mind is usually exhausted after visiting Nowhere.

Now Here

When the Mind is at Now Here it is surrounded by purposeful, positive and powerful thoughts.
Now Here has loads of new perspectives and the Mind can even meet Creativity here.
Once Creativity and Mind become good friends they can do loads of new stuff together.
Mind can also visit Happiness here. Happiness only stays at Now Here.
Now Here is the best place for the Mind to be; it feels alert and alive here.

If the Mind does not know where it is going, it will for sure end up in Nowhere.
Anyway, the road from Nowhere to Now Here is pretty straight.
Mind just needs to hop on Mindfulness, give it a kick-start and drive straight to Now Here.

Life is a pilgrimage to nowhere, from nowhere to nowhere.
And between these two nowheres is the Now-Here.
Osho

Try this: Whatever you are doing stop for a moment right now. Bring all your attention to the present moment. Notice your breath going in and out. Feel the sensation of inhaling and exhaling... Become fully present and be here now.

Escaping

When we face extremely stressful situations we just want to escape. Sometimes we escape by using maladaptive coping strategies.

Sleeping too much, drinking too much alcohol, eating too much, watching TV all the time, Netflix bingeing, impulsive shopping…

When we use these types of avoidance practices, in order to cope, in the long run they are even more damaging to us than the stressful situation itself.

Diversion

When we face extreme stress it is better to divert our attention towards something different but positive. Example: going for an aerobics class, meeting friends and talking about something different, joining a sports group, learning something new, cooking for a friend, creating artwork, making crafts, writing a story, practising yoga…

When we use these types of positive diversions rather than negative coping strategies we can proactively reduce our stress plus enhance our well-being.

Drinking, gambling, bingeing, gaming…

Instead of doing the wrong type of coping, use a positive diversion.

Exercising, cooking, learning…

In periods of stress and disarray a diversion will feel bothersome, as you will have so many other things on your mind.

However, once you engage with a particular positive activity, the diversion will take you to the road of recovery.

When you face extreme stress in your life, try to do something positive to divert your mind.

A diversion in your journey can take you to a different path and you can enjoy a new scenery for a while, until you get back to your main road.

Do: Make a list of your positive diversions. Keep your 'Diversion list' handy. Next time you face some severe stress instead of the wrong type of coping use a diversion. Make your list personal. Write down all the things that you think make you feel better. Ideas: Run for 40 minutes, go for a bike ride, bake a cake, take a bubble bath, call ______ (name specific person), watch ______ (name specific movie/inspiration talk that inspires you), read ______ (name your specific book)...

Cave

Sometimes we withdraw from the crowds and go into our cave.
We disconnect and shut out other people. No one can reach us and we don't ask for help.
Being in a cave is about hating the outside world and not wanting to participate in life.
It's like putting ourselves in confinement.
A cave is isolated, cold and dark.
A cave is not a nice place to be.

Retreat

Time to time it is good to be in a quiet and calm place. It is good to withdraw from the noise and hustle and bustle of life.
This quiet time alone is like a retreat. It does not mean you have to book yourself on some expensive exotic spa retreat package. It just means treating your alone time like a retreat.
Some alone time is necessary for refreshing and renewing your energies.

What is your alone time like, a cave or a retreat?
Going into a cave means you hate the outside world and want to shut it out.
Being in a retreat means you feel blessed to be a part of a beautiful world and you just want to withdraw for a while so you can appreciate it from a distance.

Going into a cave means shutting out the present.
Going into a retreat means silencing the past and future and becoming fully present.

Do: Design yourself a mini retreat. For a few hours or a couple of days, plan to be alone. Detach from all social media, TV, phones… have a relaxing bath, drink some fresh juice, listen to soothing instrumental music, meditate… read this book☺, become fully present and appreciate and reflect on all the amazing and beautiful things of your life…

Virtual Reality

Quite a lot of what we do now is online.
We live in a digital era.
Whatever we do online and whatever happens online also affects us in our real life.
All technology has some level of impact on us and our experiences; therefore it is all a part of our experienced reality.
Nothing is just virtual reality...

Augmented Reality

Whatever we experience in this world is partly enhanced or affected by our own internal filters. We actually don't see the world 100% accurately; it is modified by our own perception of reality.
Everything we live and experience is our own interpretation. We add our own meaning to all situations.
Everything is augmented reality...

All new technologies are bringing loads of new creative ways to see and interact with the world.
The gaps between reality, augmented reality and virtual reality are rapidly decreasing.
It is even more important now not to forget to nurture our own inner cyber sense.

Augmented reality technology can enhance the perception of our current surroundings and Virtual reality can even try to replace it, but Reality is what we feel and live individually.
It starts with us and ends with us and not with some technology.

Do: Try to experience Virtual reality and Augmented reality...
How do you feel about each, really?

Discharge

We know very well that all our gadgets discharge with constant usage. They lose battery power as we use them. We also know that running many programs at the same time on the computer depletes its battery power quicker. Also our mobile phones discharge quicker when we have too many apps open at the same time.

We know how quickly our gadgets discharge. Do we know how quickly our inner energy of positivity discharges during the day?

Charge

We charge our mobile phones every day. We make sure that the battery power does not run out during the day. We also carry extra chargers with us. We consciously keep an eye on our phone's battery level during the day.

We are aware of charging our gadgets, but are we aware of charging ourselves with positive energy every day?

Just like our gadgets, our inner positive energy can deplete during the day.

We can feel mental exhaustion.

It is important to charge this inner positive energy daily.

Few quiet moments on our own with inner silence can help us recharge our inner power.

Learn to replenish your inner positive energy by charging your spiritual battery every day.

Just like you charge your phone daily.

You would not want your phone to run out of battery power during the day.

So how can you allow yourself to be depleted and discharged of all inner positivity?

Try this: When you notice that your inner energy is low, you are starting to get irritated or demotivated, sit in silence with a quiet mind for a few moments. Replenish your inner positive energy. You can also do other things to recharge your inner energy... go for a walk, cook, listen to music... read something positive...

ACHE

It's awful to have a strong headache or any other type of ache somewhere in your body.
If you could give your ache to your best friend, would you?
An ache is not a nice thing to give to others.

CAKE

It is nice to have a slice of your favourite cake.
If you could share your yummy cake with your friend, wouldn't you?
It is so enjoyable to share your yummy cake with your friends.

Everyone likes to have a slice of a yummy cake.
No one likes aches.

Share your C.A.K.E – Compassion, Appreciation, Kindness, Empathy.
Not your A.C.H.E – Anger, Complaints, Hate, Envy.

Try this: Invite a friend to come and watch a comedy film. Make or buy a cake she/he likes. Enjoy the cake and the film and your friendship.

Motivation

Having Money

Everyone wants more money. Some people think having loads of money in their bank account will make them happy.
Having loads of money does not guarantee happiness or love.
It is good to have the ambition to acquire wealth... but true wealth does not only mean having loads of money.

Being Wealthy

Being wealthy is not so much about money, it is about your attitude in life. Being wealthy is also a relative term. To a beggar, who does not have money for a single meal, a person with a regular job can appear rich.
In someone's eyes out there, you are already wealthy so start considering yourself wealthy. Start counting your true wealth – your family, your friends, your health, your environment...

Don't wait to have millions in your bank account to be wealthy.
Wealthy is what wealthy does.
Be wealthy now, be generous, be giving.

A man's true wealth hereafter is the good he has done to his fellowmen.
Mahatma Gandhi

Idea: For a day, imagine yourself to be a very wealthy person, but you mustn't spend any money at all on the day. How would you behave towards others?

Functional

Functional is when everything is OK but nothing is great.
It is about getting by, somehow.
It is about survival and about just making do.
It is about remaining just above 0. Not in the minus but not progressing towards plus either.

Flourishing

Flourishing is when life is beyond OK... It feels great!
It is about thriving in spite of all the problems. It is about using the difficulties in life as a stepping stone for greater and better things to come.
Flourishing means growing and progressing in all situations.
It means moving from 0 towards +10.

Flourishing means to be who you are meant to be and not just remain a product of your circumstances.

A lotus flower flourishes in the murkiest of situations. It uses the nutrients in the mud for its growth.

Exercise: Describe your 'mud'. What hardships have you faced in your life? What nourishment did they provide you for your growth?

Sphere of Silly

Sphere of silly is filled with things that you don't have any control over yet they preoccupy you.
Politicians, celebrity lives, what other people think, weather, tabloid press, neighbour gossip, supermodels, boss' car...
In this sphere a lot of time and energy is wasted.

Sphere of Significance

Sphere of significance is filled with things that are meaningful and directly relevant to your life.
Your values, your attitude, how you live, what work you do, what you read, how you are with your friends, how you deal with mistakes... your strengths...
Sphere of significance is where you should be spending most of your time.

The sphere of silly should be about the size of a pea.
Sphere of significance comparatively should be like a huge watermelon.

Don't waste time on things that don't matter.
You can get plenty of things that don't matter everywhere anytime.
What you cannot get back is your time.

Exercise: Draw two circles. Put all your time-wasting activities in one and all important and meaningful activities in the other one. Over the next few days try to make the circle with wasteful activities smaller and the other one bigger.

Security

We all want to feel secure. We all want a guarantee that things will turn out OK.
We think we can obtain this guarantee by getting a stable job, a mortgage, a car… We think that a regular salary will give us this security. Hence the salary becomes our security.
We feel afraid to lose this salary and we tie ourselves to the job, for the sake of security.
Then as time passes by, we start complaining that the job has taken away our freedom. We start dreaming about what we would be doing if we were not tied to the job…

Freedom

Freedom is not just about civil liberty nor is it just about independence.
It is also not just about doing what you want whenever you want.
Freedom is about the chance to take a shot at your dreams.
Many people go through life without actually ever taking a real chance towards achieving their dreams. They don't allow themselves the freedom. They get too stuck in the rut of life that they think that doing what you want is for 'other' people, people who are 'free' from responsibilities…

Often we use security as a scapegoat for the price of our freedom.
It's not about security, it is about permission.
When you allow yourself to take a real chance towards your dreams you give yourself the freedom.

Greatest freedom is the freedom we allow our own selves to be who we are meant to be.

Do: Take a sheet of paper and just randomly write down all that you want to do in life. Don't put anything in any sort of order, priority or significance. Just scribble away… put the paper away and look at it after a few days. Which things are standing out distinctly?

Why me?

'Why me' attitude is dangerous. It passively takes one towards a downwards spiral of self-pity, doubt, shame and helplessness. Once you are going down that spiral everything seems to work against you.
Why do bad things happen to me all the time? Why is everything against me?
Why me… keeps us stuck in the past…

Try me!

When you feel a 'Why me?' coming on just change it to – Try me!
Just say to yourself, 'Whatever is happening is good. It is a special challenge for me to trigger bigger and better things to come.'
'Try me' is proactive… it leads to What's next? What can I do…? How can I…?
Try me… moves us forward…

Next time something happens to you and you ask yourself, 'Why me?' just immediately tell yourself, this is a 'Try me!' moment. Whatever has appeared does not look nice, but it is a trigger for something better ahead.

A victim always asks, Why me?
A champion says, Try me!

Think about: One negative thing that happened to you in the past few years… What other things followed that which became triggers for better changes…

Always and Never

'Always' and 'Never' statements are rarely true.
We all make statements such as:
I always listen to you.
You never listen to me.
He always criticizes me.
She never agrees with me.
It is not true that you have always listened to your partner, your friend has never listened to you ever, your boss has never praised you about anything, your sister has never agreed with you on anything...

Sometimes

We all know that sometimes others can be less attentive towards us and likewise sometimes we can also be less attentive to needs of others around us.
It is good to remember that 'sometimes' is more realistic than 'always' and 'never'.
'Sometimes' is softer and more true-to-life.

In reality always and never are rare. Sometimes statements are more correct.
It's good to check our statements before making them.

Sometimes you laugh, sometimes you cry, sometimes you are sad, sometimes you are happy, sometimes you get lucky... 'Sometimes' happens more times in life than anything else.

Suggestion: Check your 'always' and 'never' statements. Some can be turned into 'sometimes' statements.

Responsibility

Responsibilities are things that we have to deal with. They are things we are accountable for. They are our obligations.
At times our responsibilities feel like heavy burdens or restraints.
'Gosh, I have so much responsibility… I am exhausted, phew!'

Response-ability

Response-ability is not a burden it's a privilege. It is your ability to choose your response. This gives you choice and autonomy. Whenever you are dealing with something you are responsible for, just remind yourself… 'This is my privilege as I have the ability to choose my response towards this.'

Response-ability is a gift to yourself.
It is your ability to choose your response towards any situation.
Be response-able towards your responsibilities.

Don't be weighed down by your responsibilities.
Be set free by your response-ability.

Exercise: List three things you are responsible for in your daily life. See these responsibilities as privileges. Choose the best possible response for situations related to them.

Handyman

Handyman fixes things that are damaged in the house.
Handyman focuses on repairing stuff.

Architect

Architect is someone who designs new houses and buildings.
Architect focuses on creating new buildings.

Are you a handyman or architect of your life?
Do you live your life just repairing, rectifying, fixing old stuff?
Or are you designing, creating, growing new things?

Psychology should be as concerned with building strengths as with repairing damage.
Martin Seligman

Idea: Pick three of your qualities (e.g. Kindness, Honesty, Zest, Forgiveness, Open-mindedness, Bravery, Humour, Modesty etc.). Think about activities and interactions that will help you to use and strengthen these specific qualities.

Lost

Something is lost when it cannot be found or retrieved. Feeling lost in life means feeling that everything has been a waste and there is no way out of the present situation. Everything seems aimless. It is a feeling of helplessness and defeat. Feeling lost is not good.

Wandering

Sometimes we all feel like we are wandering around looking for our right path. We don't know where we are going, but we are actively looking. Wandering is different from being lost. Wandering is not about aimlessness, it is about searching. When we seek, we shall find.

Allow yourself to wander a little.
Learn new things, taste new foods, watch films that are not your usual choice...
Explore a little...
Wandering does not mean you are lost, it means you are searching.
When you search, you will find!

Each of us needs to withdraw from the cares which will not withdraw from us.
We need hours of aimless wandering or spates of time sitting on park benches,
observing the mysterious world of ants and the canopy of treetops.
Maya Angelou

Suggestion: Spend a day with no plan. Just wander about in the city and look around and go with the flow and explore. At the end of the day list all the new things you saw, came across, discovered... learned...

Restless

Some people are always going somewhere, doing something, attending something, meeting someone, updating something… they are hardly ever still.
They are always occupied with some activity or another.
When they are eating lunch with one friend, they will be messaging another one. When they are on holiday they will be doing some work stuff. When they are at work they will be checking out their next holiday destination…
Restless people are so impatient that they are not fully present in any situation.

Being Active

Being active does not mean you have to constantly be planning your next activity before one finishes. Being active is not about filling the diary. Nor is it continuous extension of activities back to back.
Being active means being engaged with meaningful pursuits and being fully present whilst carrying them out.
It means being actively involved with what you are doing and giving it your full attention.
Active people have a lot of patience and are rarely seen rushing about.

Are you so addicted to activity that an empty schedule makes you restless?
Are you more concerned about filling up the diary than enjoying the activity itself?
Are you just restless or are you active?

Restless people go to many events but they never fully attend anything.

Do: Next time you meet a friend for lunch or dinner, switch your phone off for the entire time you are with them. Don't check it at all; give your full attention to your friend.

Compulsion

Compulsion is something we just 'have' to do.
Sometimes we tie ourselves to an objective and we get so fixated by it that it becomes a compulsive obligation. It can make us aggressive and sometimes even hostile. It becomes a restraint.
It feels like a heavy iron ball tied to the leg by a chain.

Aspiration

Aspiration is something we want to achieve. It is something that drives us and motivates us. It is something we dream of accomplishing.
It makes us feel enthusiastic about life. It leads us forwards. It is fun and feels like a skateboard.

If you feel you are constantly dragging yourself with a heavy load in order to achieve your goals... re-examine your aspirations... they may turn out to be your compulsions.

Are your goals turning into your compulsions?
Do they still inspire you?

Do: Examine your aims, goals, objectives and aspirations... Which of them are starting to feel like heavy loads? What can you change about them? Which ones can you let go of?

Shaken

Feeling shaken is when something negative happens in life and it manages to completely take away your inner stability. You get so affected by the problem at hand that you are not able to see anything beyond it. You remain agitated and disturbed by it and cannot make yourself stable. When you are shaken other areas of your life are also affected negatively.

Stirred

Not all negative events have a bad outcome. Sometimes the purpose of a negative event is to stir us in order to make other things happen.

Feeling stirred is when the negative event gives you the stimulation to do something positive. It prompts you take positive action and moves you forward.

We can use the negative events that happen in our life to stir us positively.

It is good to build positive mental resilience so that when something negative happens in life, it does not have the power to shake you completely.
It only stirs you positively.

Might be better to shake and not stir the martinis...
But as far as life is concerned it is better to be stirred but not shaken.

Suggestion: Watch a controversial film. Write down all the thoughts that were stirred by watching the film. Think about channelling them in a positive direction.

Change

Change does not always mean we are moving in the right direction. Sometimes we think we are creating change but in fact we are just altering the camouflage and nothing else.
It is like when you change your television set but continue watching the same programs on the new one.
You can go and live in a new country, but all you will be altering is just your surroundings. If you don't manage to change your perceptions, your attitudes and your thoughts you might be changing the location but you end up looking at the same scenery.

Progress

Progress means growth.
Things take time to grow. There are no quick fixes.
When we feel stuck or we are in a negative place we want things to change. We often go for quick fixes to create change.
Get a new hairstyle, move into a new area, and change your job... change your partner, change your car... etc.
Nothing wrong with changing stuff, but if you are just altering the external stuff without any internal growth then not much will really progress.

Quick fix is not progress. Progress needs effort and determination. For real progress, change the beliefs that hold you back, change your negative attitude, not just your hairstyle or your car.

Change is inevitable, it occurs in the universe automatically.
It is involuntary.
Progress happens only with effort and determination, it is not automatic.
It is voluntary.

Think about: Two things that you changed recently. Which led to real progress?

Plasticity

Plasticity means whatever situations arise in life, we mould ourselves to fit into them.
We also modify ourselves to how other people want us to be.
Sometimes we alter ourselves so much for situations and other people that we forget our original form.
Situations or people should not make us forget who we are inside.

Elasticity

Elasticity means we are able to stretch ourselves when we are in tough situations or with demanding people. We are able to adapt and adjust.
It also means we retain the ability to return to our original authentic self.
So no matter what happens in life, we have the ability to return to our core values and qualities. Nothing on the outside has the power to take us away from our original true self.

Remaining flexible is an important quality in life.
Flexibility does not mean losing who we are. It means having the ability to adjust to the situation but not to lose touch with your core self.
It means having the ability to be your authentic self in all situations.

Don't be Plastic, be Elastic!
The quality of Elasticity allows us the ability to stretch and expand our awareness,
yet retains the sensibility to come back to the core self at any moment.

Think about: A situation where you sacrificed a core value. How did that make you feel? How could you have done it differently? How could you have offered flexibility to the situation but not compromised your integrity?

Dreams

We have dreams when we are sleeping. Dreams consist of random imagery that occurs involuntarily during certain stages of sleep.
We see random places and people in our dreams. Some dreams we remember and some we forget. Nobody can say for sure what dreams mean.

Revelations

Revelations happen when we are awake. We get sudden ideas or thoughts that reveal something to us. It is important not to ignore these personal disclosures.
These ideas and thoughts uncover some of our un-acted wishes. They reveal some needs that we are neglecting. What do they tell us about ourselves?

When you get a sudden idea about something,
Think about what it is revealing to you.
Is it something you are neglecting?
Something you were meant to do, somewhere you were meant to be…

The revelation of thought takes men out of servitude into freedom.
Ralph Waldo Emerson

Think about: Do you have an idea that keeps popping up? What is it telling you?

Comfort Zone

Being comfortable is nice; feeling uncomfortable is not that nice.
We all like to be comfortable. It makes us feel safe. Feeling safe is about familiarity and doing the things we have always done. When we keep doing the things that we have always done, we also only experience the things we have always experienced. Then we complain that nothing ever changes.

Stretch Zone

Sometimes to achieve our goals we have to exit our comfort zone. We have to try new things. New things that are not familiar to us can make us feel uncomfortable. A little discomfort when trying something new is OK.
This does not mean abandoning all our comforts completely; it just means expanding our circle of familiarity.

Comfort zone is about routine, patterns, familiarity... It is about doing what you have always done.
It is good to be comfortable, but to bring about positive change we have to stretch a little bit.
Stretch zone lies just a bit outside the comfort zone. It is where growth happens.
Don't let your comforts imprison you.
Step outside the cage from time to time to discover what lies on the outside...

The lust for comfort murders the passions of the soul.
Kahlil Gibran

Do: On a blank sheet of paper draw a big circle and inside it drawn a smaller inner circle. List all the things that you currently do in the inner circle. In the outer circle list all the things you would like to do and dream of doing. The inner circle is your comfort zone, the outer circle is your stretch zone...

To-Do List

We all have a 'to-do list'. Some write it on paper, some put it on their digital calendar, some just have it in their head... no matter how we keep it, we all have it.

A 'to-do list' helps us to organize our time and helps us to remember what needs to be done.

- Buy toothpaste
- Fix the broken chair
- Book an appointment with the dentist
- Prepare for staff meeting

To-Be List

A 'to-be list' is a list to remind us how we need to be whilst doing the things we need to do. It helps us to remember and use our internal qualities.

All tasks and interactions need different qualities.

- Be calm when kids make a mess
- Be kind to the new neighbour
- Be patient in the traffic jam
- Be enthusiastic in the staff meetings

To-do list is about the things we have to do. We need to know the time and day to do them.

All things we have to do also need a different quality.

Some need patience, some need strength, others need energy...

When we apply the right quality to the right task,
things not only get done but they get done very well.

To-be list reminds you how to be, whilst you do...
Example: Whenever you are going to be doing something new, you can add 'be courageous' to your to-be list.

Exercise: Write down your 'to-be list' and keep it in a place where you can look at it regularly.

Fight It

Fighting is about attack. It is about confronting and opposing the situation and proving it wrong.

Fighting generally makes situations even worse.

Fighting is about pointing out the wrongs of the other person.

The aim of a fight is to win.

Face It

Facing something is about acknowledging the part we play in it.

The aim of facing something is to have the best outcome for the situation or people involved, even if it means losing your argument.

Facing it is about owning up to your faults.

Fighting something or someone is about your ego.
Facing something is about your courage to accept the role you played in the situation.

What you see in others is also perhaps inside of you.
Face it, what's around you is a reflection of what's inside of you.

Suggestion: Next time you are in a disagreement about something, before fighting it, try to analyse what part you played in making that situation worse...

Self-Deceit

Self-deceit is about deceiving our own self. It is about hiding behind excuses and not facing the truth.
- The long-term traveller who proclaims a passion for travelling but in reality wants to escape responsibility.
- The workaholic who is avoiding relationship issues.
- The regular social drinker who is not facing the drinking problem.

Self-Belief

Self-belief is about believing in yourself. It comes from knowing your own self very well.
- The person who says, 'I love travelling,' and really does it for the love of discovery and not as an excuse for running away from responsibility.
- The person who says, 'I am passionate about the work I do,' works a lot because they love it and not because they want to hide behind it in order to avoid relationships.

Self-belief is about knowing yourself and what you tell yourself. Whatever you tell yourself usually becomes either your self-belief or your self-deceit.

Whether you think you can, or you think you can't – you're right.
Henry Ford

Think about: Are there any self-deceits hiding in your cupboard?

Willpower

Willpower is the ability to control our impulses. It is the ability to resist temptation.
At times it feels like we have to fight against the tide of temptation or opposing circumstance in order to stick to our goals.
Fighting against the tide or the current can be tiring and exhausting.

Wave power

Wave power is obtained by harnessing the energy produced by the waves at sea. The more windy and turbulent the sea gets the more energy is captured.
It might be helpful to think of willpower as wave power… the more wind blows the more energy is produced.
We need to learn to ride the waves and use the ups and downs of life to provide momentum to go forward.

No matter how much willpower you have, you cannot control the entire ocean.
Learn to ride the waves and generate wave power.
Use the momentum of the ups and downs of life to give you the power to move forward.

Willpower is about resisting or fighting temptation and circumstances.
Wave power is not about fighting, it's about using the turbulence to generate momentum in the right direction.

Suggestion: Identify a role model that demonstrates perseverance and willpower. Read about their journey and find out how they used adversity in their life to move forward.

Get Busy Disappearing

As our age progresses, we start letting go of our dreams. We put them aside and no longer consider them our priority. We start to get busy disappearing and fading... We get busy preparing for a life that is declining.

Old age may mean slowing down but it does not mean stagnation to the point where you disappear from life much before life disappears...

Get Busy Living

When you continue to pursue what you love and don't let your visions and aspirations disappear just because of your age you are truly living to the full.

Life is about living to the full, regardless of your age.

Get busy living no matter how old you are.

Living life fully is about growing and learning until the day we die.

Just because your eyesight starts to decline with age does not mean you start fading away from life yourself.

Do: Think about hobbies/activities you loved doing few years ago but you stopped doing them now because you feel too old for them. Think about which two activities you could continue doing regardless of age.

Must Do

When we 'must do' something, it is like a liability. It feels heavy and burdensome.

I must exercise daily
I must study more
I must eat healthier

Also, with other people must-do statements are like ordering them.

You must call me
You must pick me up
You must tell me...

Could Do

Could do is an option not an obligation. It feels lighter.

I could exercise daily
I could study more
I could eat healthier

With other people, a could-do statement gives them the choice.

You could call me
You could pick me up
You could tell me...

'Must do' is an order to yourself and others. 'Could do' is a suggestion.
It is better when someone does things they feel they want to do rather than feel they have to do.

Don't give yourself an ultimatum, give yourself permission. Change 'I must', 'I should' to 'I could.'

Try this: Observe your language, note instances when you use must and should. Replace them with 'could'...

Obsession

Obsession is an unhealthy fixation that takes over your ability to reason.
It is something that controls you rather than you controlling it.
It causes conflict with other activities and aspects of your life.
Obsession to become a pop star.
Obsessed with going to the gym.

Passion

Passion is a strong inclination toward something. It is something we like to do and find important. We engage with it willingly.
Passion enhances other aspects of life.
Passion for singing.
Passion for exercise and good health.

Obsession is persistent preoccupation with something that makes our live difficult.
Passion is the driving force that makes our lives more meaningful.

Develop not just the courage to follow your passions but also the strength not to be controlled by your obsessions.

Do: Make a list of your passions and your obsessions.

Push-goal

A push goal is something that you have to force yourself to do.
It's hard to get motivated about it.
'I must lose weight', 'I should go to the gym everyday'...
Although there is nothing wrong with these, they put pressure on you emotionally as they are mostly driven by guilt. They are not natural and you have to constantly push yourself towards them.
Constant pushing gets emotionally draining. When we get drained emotionally we usually give up on the goal.

Pull-goal

Some goals or aspirations feel natural and easy and you are automatically drawn to them.
You don't have to push yourself towards them.
They are intrinsic and driven by motivations such as happiness, joy, peace, love.
They are guilt free.
'I love being healthy', 'I enjoy daily exercise'...
These goals are emotionally fulfilling, and when we feel emotionally fulfilled we are more likely to succeed in achieving them.

It is much easier to be pulled towards something than to force yourself on something.

Observe your goals.
Are you pushing a heavy load on the wheelbarrow or is a beautiful carriage driving you.

Think about: Which things you do in daily life that feel like heavy loads? Also think about the things that you are naturally drawn to.

Limiting Belief

Limiting beliefs are beliefs we have about ourselves that hold us back and limit us in many ways.

- I am clumsy, I cannot dance.
- I am unattractive.
- I am not clever.

Sometimes a limiting belief can be so deep rooted in us that we don't even realize that it's there.

Power Belief

Once we discover our limiting belief, we can transform it and make it a power belief.

Example: Transform, 'I cannot dance' to 'I am able to improve the way I dance with some practice.'

Power beliefs help to transform what we thought was fixed and unchangeable into something we are able to change.

Power beliefs help us to remove internal blocks and assist us in making positive progress.

Step one is to identify and become aware of your limiting beliefs. Step two is to think about the consequences of your limiting belief. Step three is to transform the limiting belief to an appropriate power belief.

Limiting beliefs are like a barbed wire fence. They keep us in confinement.

Exercise: Identify a limiting belief; think how this limiting belief is affecting your life. Transform this limiting belief into a power belief.

Actions

In some relationships we do everything right yet the relationship seems stuck.
We say and do nice things for the other person, we give compliments, we buy presents, we talk to them nicely etc. yet the relationship does not progress and feels uncomfortable.
We keep wondering why that person is so difficult and awkward...

Intention

Saying and doing nice things for someone is not enough.
What we actually think and feel about the other person inside contributes to the energy of the overall relationship.
It is about having good thoughts and feelings for them inside.
When we really have only good thoughts for someone and our intentions are pure towards them, the quality of the energy of the relationship with them will be positive, regardless how they are towards us.

Imagine this: You buy a friend an expensive present for his/her birthday.
Inside you secretly hope to be more popular or look better than him/her at their birthday party.
At the end of the evening you complain, 'I gave him/her such an expensive present but he/she was so awkward towards me the whole evening...'
The quality of the energy of your interactions starts with your internal intention.
Our thoughts and intentions have to be pure and positive first.

Words and actions can only be authentic when they are backed by honest and clear intentions.
It is what we really feel and think inside about someone that creates better relationships rather than actions or words alone.

Try this: When you are doing something nice or saying something nice to someone, also observe the quality of your deeper intentions.

I wish...

I wish...
I wish I could travel for a year.
I wish I had my own business.
I wish I had a job that I like.
I wish...
When we say 'I wish' we actually don't believe it could happen and we just keep dreaming about it, and it is no more than just wishful thinking.

I will!

I will is about having faith in yourself.
I will travel for a year.
I will start my own business.
I will find a job that I like.
Saying 'I will' is a declaration to yourself. It confirms the courage to believe something and the determination to do it.

'I wish' means you just passively dream for something to happen or someone to appear and provide you with what you want. 'I will' is a declaration to yourself to go after what you want.

There is a difference between wishing for a thing and being ready to receive it.
No one is ready for a thing, until he believes he can acquire it.
Napoleon Hill

Exercise: Write down all the statements that you regularly say starting with 'I wish'... Which of these statements are real desires that lack courage and action?

Good Old Days

Some people are always moaning about the present and yearning for the 'good old days'.
They keep repeating how everything was so much better 'back then' and how everything is getting worse nowadays.
What is the point of wanting things to be exactly as they were in the past?
Past is gone. Things change.

Nowadays

Nowadays are the days we are living.
If you think and act like 'nowadays' is not a good place to be then remember that in years to come these days will become your 'good old days'.
Make 'nowadays' good days and stop wasting time longing for some bygone era.

What good old days? The Holocaust, World Wars, Slavery, Epidemics...?
The past was not all good and the present is not all bad...
The reality is that some things were good then, but some things are better now.

'Nowadays' of one generation will be 'good old days' of another generation.
Make 'nowadays' count for everyone.

Suggestion: Talk to someone who is always complaining about the present and praising the past. Ask them what were the bad things of the past and what are the good things about the present.

Talent

Some people are talented singers, actors, footballers... Sometimes people think that the talent itself is the aim of life. Singing, acting, playing football is what they live for.

Tool

Talents are just tools.
Everyone has a different tool.
All tools are used in different ways.
The purpose of a tool is to do something useful by utilising it. It is not just an ornament.
Your tool enables you to give to others in your own unique way.

A talent is a strength, a quality, a special ability, an attribute...
Each and every one of us has something special.
It may not be a super talent but it could be a quiet internal strength that is unique to us.

Talent is the tool and not the aim of life itself.
The aim of life is to give. Use your tool to give to others.

Exercise: Think of a quality within you that you can call a talent.
How can you use it to help others?

Survive

Sometimes we live life as if its aim is just to survive.
Surviving is about focusing just on our own needs. We do things just for our own existence. We go to our job to pay for our car and our house. The car that we only need to get to the job and the house that we leave empty all day to be at the job.
We work to pay our bills and to buy the things that we may not even need in the first place...
Surely there is more to life than just surviving.

Serve

Life is about serving others and not just surviving for our own sake.
When we live to give and share whatever we have with others, life becomes more than just mere existence. It becomes purposeful and meaningful.
When we live to serve and contribute to others, everything we do becomes significant and important no matter how mundane it may be.
When we focus on giving and serving the motivation of our life changes. Life becomes much more than just survival.

Life is not just about survival but also about contribution.
By serving others we contribute to the greater good.
The greater good is what connects us all.

The best way to find yourself is to lose yourself in the service of others.
Mahatma Gandhi

Exercise: Today do two acts of random kindness for strangers. See how you feel afterwards.

Boiled Frog

If you put a frog into a pan of water and slowly heat the water, the frog will keep adjusting to the rising temperature. It adapts to the rising temperature so much that it boils to death. It does not perceive the danger of the slowly rising temperature.

Similarly when we keep making sacrifices to our inner being in order to meet the requirements of the situation we have to be careful.

Over-adaptation can happen in relationships or at work, when we adjust to something or someone's incorrect behaviour so much so that we eventually sacrifice our own sense of being and our values.

Bouncing Frog

If you throw boiling water at a frog, it will immediately perceive danger. It will bounce away from it.

When a situation arises where you have to let go of your inner values and standards, it is better to jump out.

Sometimes in a relationship or a job a person thinks they can adjust their moral standards just a little bit to please the situation. However, if they continuously keep adjusting in the end they will have completely sacrificed their values and their own sense of being.

Don't stay in bad relationships or less than adequate job conditions; recognize what's not good for you. Jump out at the right time!

Slowly rising temperatures are harder to detect.
Tune in to your inner barometer regularly to get an accurate reading.
Build awareness of what is right for you and what is not.

Sometimes little things can build up so slowly that you won't realize until it's too late.
Don't neglect the little things, take care of them.
Don't end up a boiled frog.

Think about: In the past did you ever sacrifice your own values for someone else? Did you end up doing things that did not seem right according to your inner value system? What were the consequences?

Finding Time

Do you struggle to find time when a good friend needs your help?

When a good friend needs your help but you struggle to find time, then it is not really about the time, it is about your own priorities.

It is not a nice thing to make someone special feel that when they need your help you don't really have any time for them.

Being Available

Being available means that your friends and family know that you will be there for them when they are faced with some difficulty and need your help. Being available does not mean having nothing to do and having loads of free time all the time. It just means not to get so hung up on protecting your time that you are not available to the important people in your life in their time of need.

Don't be stingy with your time.
The only thing you do have in this very moment is time.
If you had no time left, you would actually be dead.
A friend in need is a friend indeed.
Be available, don't just find time.

If you don't find time for your friends, soon you won't find any friends.

Do: Send this message to an elderly friend or relative –
'Hi, I am available for the whole day/afternoon/evening on _______! I can go anywhere or do whatever you would like…'

To Me

When something adverse or negative happens, do you automatically say or think things such as:

It's all going wrong for me!

Everything turns out against me!

All negative things happen to me!

For Me

When you feel everything is happening to you, turn it around and say to yourself everything is actually happening 'for me'. 'There is benefit in this for me.'

This means there is some new opportunity opening up through whatever is happening.

If you keep thinking that everything is against you, you'll be stuck in the negativity mode.

Start believing that whatever happens, happens for good.

Then automatically everything will start happening 'for you'.

Everything that happens highlights or teaches us something.

It contributes to our growth.

It helps us to become who we are meant to be.

Everything happens for you.

Try this: Turn something negative that you feel is happening 'to me' into 'for me'.

Think about just one sentence to explain why it is good for you.

______ is happening. Actually this is good for me because _________.

Get Over It

When we experience something negative we are told to get over it.
Getting over something means to carry on as if it did not happen, and not allow it to affect us; and to remove it from our hearts and minds completely. Getting over something is like trying to make a clean jump over a large muddy puddle.

Get Through It

Getting through it means to allow ourselves to acknowledge the pain and hurt of the negative experience.
Getting through it means walking through the muddy puddle barefoot.
Allowing the feet to sink in the mud. Feeling the mud under the feet and continuing to walk across the puddle.

We cannot always get over it. Sometimes we just have to get through it.
Getting through it means having the courage to feel the pain and yet remaining optimistic for the future.

It is not a good idea to try to jump across all the large muddy puddles
that we come across in life.
Sometimes we just have to walk through them with bare feet, feeling the mud.

Think about: A past painful experience. How did you deal with it at the time? What were you saying to yourself during that time? How were you feeling?

Living Life

Living a life is about doing things because you have to do them.
It is about carrying on somehow and doing what needs to be done.
Are you alive for just earning a living?

Loving Life

Loving life is to love the things you do.
It is a little bit more than just doing.
It is about injecting love and joy in doing, no matter how small the task is.
Are you creating a loving life?

Loving life means being enthusiastic about each and every single day.
It is about creating joy even where there is none.

Not all of us can do great things, but we can all do small things with great love.
Mother Teresa

Try this: Today make a cup of tea for someone... do it with great love!
All the big or small things you do for others, do them with joy, create a loving life!

Suggested Reading

Ben-Shahar, T. (2007) *Happier*. New York: McGraw-Hill.

Boniwell, I. (2008) *Positive Psychology in a Nutshell (2nd Ed.)*. London: PWBC.

Dweck, CS (2006) *Mindset: The New Psychology of Success*. New York: Random House.

Kabat-Zinn, J. (1990) *Wherever You Go, There You Are: Mindfulness Meditation for Everyday Life*. New York: Hyperion.

Matthews, A. (1998) *Being Happy!* Singapore: Media Masters.

Peterson, C. (2006) *A Primer in Positive Psychology*. New York: Oxford University Press.

Purdie, J. (2010) *Life Coaching for Dummies*. Chichester: John Wiley & Sons.

Schwartz, B. (2004) *The Paradox of Choice: Why More Is Less*. New York: HarperCollins.

Seligman, MEP (2011) *Flourish: A Visionary New Understanding of Happiness and Well-being*. New York: Free Press.

Seligman, MEP (1991) *Learned Optimism*. New York: Knopf.

Subirana, M. (2008) *Who Rules in Your Life? Reflections on Personal Power*. New York: O-Books.

Tolle, E. (1999) *The Power of Now*. New York: Hodder & Stoughton.

Find your Balance

Mind

Head	Heart
Resources	Resourcefulness
Microscope	Telescope
Knowledge	Wisdom
Judging	Discerning
Critical thinking	Creative thinking
Daydreaming	Visualisation
Benefit	Reason
Roadblocks	Bridges
Struggling	Juggling
Outcome	Process
Fixed Mindset	Growth Mindset
Post-Traumatic Stress	Post Traumatic Growth
Why?	Why not!
Trait	State
Equal	Fair
Rigidity	Resilience
Detach	Disentangle
Black and White	Shades of Grey
Rock Bottom	Solid Foundation
Habits	Regular Activities
Copy	Original
Reducing Weaknesses	Building Strengths
Perfection	Accomplishment
Entitlement mentality	Merit mentality
Finite	Infinite
Get rid of bad thing's	Grow good things
Rationalisation	Redesign
Mindglasses	I glasses

Being understood	Explaining
Unlucky	Lucky
Lie factory	Contentment Works
Simplification	Subtraction
Certainty	Clarity
Controlling	Trusting
Love hurts	Love heals

Self-Awareness

Human doing	Human being
Living to Eat	Eating to live
Childlike	Youthful
Ideal Self	Real Self
Style	Substance
Boring	Balanced
Lonely	Alone
Passive Victim	Active Agent
Ego	Self Esteem
Success	Fulfilment
Self-sabotage	Self-sovereignty
Personality	Character
Bigotry	Banter
Self-conceited	Self-confident
Diagnosis	Prognosis
Health	Wellbeing
Explicit	Expressive
Snobbish	Stiff upper lip
Emotion	E-motion
Life Expectancy	Life Satisfaction
Self-conscious	Self-aware
Pain	Suffering
Numb	Neutralise
Delusion	Confusion

Cure	Prevention
IQ	EQ
Swallowing	Savouring
Variety	Choice
Disease	Dis-ease
Doubt	Dedication
Give up	Gain it
Comparison	Precision
Blender	Sieve
Tale of Woe	Tale of Wow
Absorbing Germs	Receiving Flowers
Rubbish Bin	Temple

Relationships

Independence	Interdependence
Stubborn	Strong
Attachment	Love
Issue	Event
Worry	Care
Hearing	Listening
Transactional Love	Unconditional Love
Sympathy	Empathy
Provoking	Evoking
Expecting	Accepting
Relationships	Relation-shifts
Neediness	Need
Obligation	Gift
Gullible	Generous
Closed Questions	Open Questions
Aggressive	Assertive
Impressing	Expressing
Forget	Forgive
Doormat	Doorman

Infatuation	Love
Sacrificing	Giving
Co-existence	Relationship
Frankness	Honesty
Relationship Busters	Relationship Boosters
Debate	Dialogue
Depreciate	Appreciate
Trial	Commitment
Changing others	Changing self
Taking Mode	Giving Mode
Tall, Dark and Harming	Tall, Dark and Handsome
Penny wise	People Foolish
Difficult People	
Teacher	Different People
Guru	
Void	Validate
Navigating	Nurturing
It's you	It's me
50 / 50	100 / 100
Soulmate	Sure mate
Yes but …	Yes and …
Letting go	Letting be
Apology	Being Sorry
Sad endings	Happy beginnings

Work Engagement

Managing	Leading
Compromise	Collaboration
Clock	Compass
Self Employed	Business owner
No Stress	Know Stress
Monetary wealth	Moral wealth
Passive Income	Automated Income

Ideas	Implementation
Turnover	Profit
Whirlwind	Propeller
Problem Talk	Solution Talk
Feedback	Feedforward
Action Faking	Action Taking
Tension	Attention
Power	Influence
Monitoring	Motivating
Unconsciously incompetent	Consciously Competent
Under Control	In Control
Activity	Productivity
Wanterprenuer	Entrepreneur
Procrastination	Postponing
Inter-personal Conflict	Intrapersonal conflict
Doing things right	Doing the right thing
Conflict Management	Facilitating Communication
Shifting responsibility	Delegating
What's not working?	What's working?
Networking	Meeting people
Earning money	Earning Blessings
Priority	Option
Monday moaning	Monday morning

Soul and Meaning

Reacting	Responding
Role Consciousness	Soul Consciousness
Self-centred	Being Centred
Outside-in	Inside-out
Meaning of life	Meaning in life
Lesson	Test
Mind - full	Mindful
Excitement	Happiness

Growing Old	Growing Up
Medication	Meditation
Nil Mind	Still Mind
Absorbing	Observing
Shelf development	Self – development
Cross roads	Roundabouts
Scarcity Mentality	Abundance Mentality
Sensibility	Sense – ability
Impulse	Instinct
Conviction	Curiosity
Blind optimism	Optimism
Tolerance	Acceptance
Careless	Carefree
Whole	Slice
Beliefs	Behaviour
Love (noun)	Love (verb)
Waiting	Patience
Intuition	In tuition
Happiness-fix	Happiness-fixed
Of this world	In this world
Beautiful	Beauty-full
Preacher	Practitioner
Listening for self.	Listening for others
Nobody	Somebody
Closed hearted	Open hearted
Weakness	Vulnerability
Trigger switch	Blessing button
Talk more	Contribute more
I want peace	I am peace
Grudge	Gratitude

Play

Be interesting	Be Interested

Until then…	Be now!
Cold	Cool
Mistakes	Missed takes
Distraction	Relaxation
IT abuse	IT use
Roller Coaster ride	Road journey
Everything	Anything
Daily action	Daily adventure
Having more	Doing more
Long Vacations	Mini Retirements
Confrontation	Challenge
Reading others mind	Minding my own business
Enjoy	In-Joy
Boldness	Courage
Coconut	Peach
Examination	Exploration
Controlling Time	Creating time
Risk	Chance
Substance abuse	Substance use
Monotony	Non-activity
Experience	Creativity
Joker	Jolly
Mr Right	Me Right
Connection	Friend
Decluttering	Minimalizing
Expensive	Valuable
Fireworks	Sparks
Nowhere	Now here
Escaping	Diversion
Cave	Retreat
Virtual Reality	Augmented Reality
Discharge	Charge
ACHE	CAKE

Motivation

Having money	Being wealthy
Functional	Flourishing
Sphere of silly	Sphere of significance
Security	Freedom
Why me?	Try me!
Always and Never	Sometimes
Responsibility	Response-ability
Handyman	Architect
Lost	Wandering
Restless	Being active
Compulsion	Aspiration
Shaken	Stirred
Change	Progress
Plasticity	Elasticity
Dreams	Revelations
Comfort Zone	Stretch Zone
To-Do list	To-Be list
Fight it	Face it
Self-Deceit	Self-Belief
Willpower	Wave power
Get busy disappearing	Get busy living
Must do	Could do
Obsession	Passion
Push-goal	Pull-goal
Limiting belief	Power belief
Actions	Intention
I wish….	I will!
Good old days	Nowadays
Talent	Tool
Survive	Serve
Boiled Frog	Bouncing Frog
Finding time	Being available

To me
Get over it
Living Life

For me
Get through it
Loving life

BOOKS

O-BOOKS

SPIRITUALITY

O is a symbol of the world, of oneness and unity; this eye represents knowledge and insight. We publish titles on general spirituality and living a spiritual life. We aim to inform and help you on your own journey in this life.

If you have enjoyed this book, why not tell other readers by posting a review on your preferred book site? Recent bestsellers from O-Books are:

Take Me To Truth

Undoing the Ego

Nouk Sanchez, Tomas Vieira

The best-selling step-by-step book on shedding the Ego, using the teachings of *A Course In Miracles*.

Paperback: 978-1-84694-050-7 ebook: 978-1-84694-654-7

The 7 Myths about Love...Actually!

The journey from your HEAD to the HEART of your SOUL

Mike George

Smashes all the myths about LOVE.

Paperback: 978-1-84694-288-4 ebook: 978-1-84694-682-0

The Message of A Course In Miracles
A translation of the text in plain language
Elizabeth A. Cronkhite
A translation of *A Course in Miracles* into plain, everyday language for anyone seeking inner peace. The companion volume, *Practicing A Course In Miracles,* offers practical lessons and mentoring.
Paperback: 978-1-84694-319-5 ebook: 978-1-84694-642-4

Your Simple Path
Find happiness in every step
Ian Tucker
A guide to helping us reconnect with what is really important in our lives.
Paperback: 978-1-78279-349-6 ebook: 978-1-78279-348-9

365 Days of Wisdom
Daily Messages To Inspire You Through The Year
Dadi Janki
Daily messages which cool the mind, warm the heart and guide you along your journey.
Paperback: 978-1-84694-863-3 ebook: 978-1-84694-864-0

Practicing A Course In Miracles
A Translation of the Workbook in Plain Language and With Mentoring Notes
Elizabeth A. Cronkhite
The practical second and third volumes of The Plain-Language *A Course In Miracles*.
Paperback: 978-1-84694-403-1 ebook: 978-1-78099-072-9

Readers of ebooks can buy or view any of these bestsellers by clicking on the live link in the title. Most titles are published in paperback and as an ebook. Paperbacks are available in traditional bookshops. Both print and ebook formats are available online.

Find more titles and sign up to our readers' newsletter at http://www.johnhuntpublishing.com/mind-body-spirit

Follow us on Facebook at https://www.facebook.com/OBooks/ and Twitter at https://twitter.com/obooks